98 Delicious Food Processor Recipes: Quick and Easy Meals for Every Occasion

Delici Food Processor

:

Contents

INTRODUCTION

Welcome to 98 Delicious Food Processor Recipes: Quick and Easy Meals for Every Occasion – a cookbook for individuals and families looking to quickly prepare delicious meals that save time and money. Offering a variety of meals and snacks from entrées and appetizers to beverages and desserts, this book is full of creative ideas and easy-to-follow instructions that make mealtime preparation a breeze.

For the busy family, this cookbook will provide a comprehensive selection of recipes that will impress the pickiest of eaters. Whip up a classic dish like spaghetti and meatballs or discover something new like a peach melba milkshake. Recipes use minimal ingredients and preparation time and feature alternative ingredients for vegan, vegetarian, gluten and dairy free diets, so everyone can enjoy a home-cooked meal or snack.

Knowing how to use a food processor is key for a successful cooking experience. This book provides comprehensive, easy-to-follow instructions on operating and caring for the food processor which will make meal preparation a snap. Additionally, this book contains helpful troubleshooting and buying tips to keep your food processor running in top notch condition.

The combination of time, money and hassle-free recipes makes this cookbook an essential addition to anyone's kitchen. Enjoy 98 Delicious Food Processor Recipes: Quick and Easy Meals for Every Occasion today, and start experiencing stress-free meal time!

1. Beef Stew with Vegetables

This hearty and flavorful Beef Stew with Vegetables is sure to satisfy! It's perfect for chilly nights and can easily be made in one pot. Serve with a side of mashed potatoes or crusty bread to mop up all the flavorful juices.

Serving: 4 to 6
| Preparation Time: 10 minutes
| Ready Time: 1 hour

Ingredients:
- 2 tablespoons of olive oil
- 2 pounds of beef stew meat, cubed
- Salt and pepper, to taste
- 1 large onion, chopped
- 4 garlic cloves, minced
- 2 tablespoons of tomato paste
- 2 cups of beef broth
- 3 tablespoons of Worcestershire sauce
- 1 large russet potato, peeled and diced
- 2 carrots, peeled and diced
- 1 cup green beans, cut into 1-inch pieces
- 2 tablespoons of fresh parsley, chopped

Instructions:
1. Heat the olive oil in a large pot over medium-high heat.
2. Season the stew meat with salt and pepper and add to the pot.
3. Cook for about 8 minutes, stirring frequently, until the meat is lightly browned.
4. Add the onion, garlic, and tomato paste and cook for another 3 minutes.
5. Add the beef broth, Worcestershire sauce, potato, carrots, and green beans.
6. Bring the stew to a boil, then reduce the heat to low and simmer, covered, for 45 minutes, stirring occasionally.
7. Remove the lid and simmer for another 15 minutes, or until the vegetables and beef are tender.
8. Stir in the parsley and season to taste with additional salt and pepper if needed.

Nutrition Information: (per serving)
Calories: 591
Fat: 27.5 grams
Protein: 60.5 grams
Carbohydrates: 21.6 grams
Fiber: 4.2 grams
Sugars: 5.3 grams
Sodium: 733 milligrams

2. Chicken Pot Pie with Puff Pastry

This classic Chicken Pot Pie with Puff Pastry is a delicious and
comforting dish! Filled with creamy chicken and vegetables in a flavorful
gravy and topped with the flakiest puff pastry, this hearty dinner will
leave your family happily satisfied.
Serving: 6-8
| Preparation Time: 15 minutes
| Ready Time: 55 minutes

Ingredients:
- 2 cups chicken, cooked & diced
- 2 tablespoons butter
- 2 stalks celery, diced
- 1 onion, minced
- 2 carrots, diced
- 2 tablespoons all-purpose flour
- 1 cup chicken broth
- 1/2 cup milk
- Salt & pepper to taste
- 1 package (17.3 oz) puff pastry, thawed

Instructions:
1. Preheat oven to 350 degrees F.
2. In medium size skillet, melt butter over medium heat. Add celery,
onion and carrot, cooking until tender, about 5-7 minutes.
3. Sprinkle the flour over the vegetables and stir to combine.
4. Pour in the chicken broth and milk, stirring continuously until the
mixture thickens, about 5 minutes.

5. Add the diced chicken, salt and pepper and mix until ingredients are fully combined.

6. Pour the chicken pot pie filling into a 9-inch baking dish.

7. Cut the puff pastry into 8 equal sized pie pieces and place over the baking dish.

8. Bake for 45-50 minutes or until the pastry is golden brown on top.

Nutrition Information:
Serving size: 1 piece
Calories: 270
Carbohydrates: 20g
Protein: 11g
Fat: 16g
Saturated Fat: 6g
Cholesterol: 20mg
Sodium: 330mg
Sugar: 1g

3. Spinach and Ricotta Ravioli

Spinach and Ricotta Ravioli are a classic Italian dish filled with luscious flavors and textures. These decadent ravioli are made with a creamy spinach and ricotta cheese filling, stuffed and wrapped into homemade pasta sheets. Whether served with a simple butter sauce or a rich ragu, this classic Italian dish is sure to be a hit with the family.

Serving: 4-6
| Preparation Time: 45 minutes
| Ready Time: 1 hour

Ingredients:
- 5 cups all-purpose flour
- 5 eggs
- 2 teaspoons olive oil
- 1/2 teaspoon salt
- Pinch of pepper
- 1 cup ricotta cheese
- 1 package frozen spinach (thawed, drained, and squeezed dry)
- 1 clove garlic (minced)

- 2 teaspoons fresh parsley (minced)
- 2 teaspoons fresh basil (minced)

Instruction:
1. In a bowl, mix together the flour, eggs, olive oil, and salt. Knead the dough until a smooth dough forms.
2. Divide the dough into four equal portions and flatten each portion into a disc.
3. Place the dough into a pasta machine and roll each disc through until it is thin. Place the dough on a lightly floured surface and cut it into circles.
4. In a bowl, mix together the ricotta cheese, spinach, garlic, parsley, and basil.
5. Spoon a tablespoon of the mixture onto the center of each dough circle and fold the dough over the filling to make a half-moon shape. Press along the edges with a fork to seal.
6. Boil the ravioli for about 4 minutes or until the ravioli begins to float.

Nutrition Information (Per serving):
Calories: 439
Fat: 13g
Carbohydrates: 64g
Protein: 15g
Sodium: 377mg
Cholesterol: 94mg

4. Lasagna with Spinach and Ricotta

Lasagna with Spinach and Ricotta is a delicious Italian dish that marries the flavors of ricotta, mozzarella, spinach, and basil for a hearty and comforting dinner.
Serves 10; | Preparation Time: 20 minutes; | Ready Time: 1 hour;

Ingredients:
1. 1 box lasagna noodles,
2. 2 tablespoons olive oil,
3. 1 onion, chopped,
4. 3 cloves garlic, minced,

5. 2 (10 ounces) packages frozen chopped spinach,
6. thawed and drained,
7. 1 cup ricotta cheese,
8. 1/2 cup grated Parmesan cheese,
9. 1/2 teaspoon salt,
10. 1/4 teaspoon freshly ground black pepper,
11. 1/4 teaspoon nutmeg,
12. 3 cups shredded mozzarella cheese;

Instructions:
1. Preheat oven to 375 degrees F.
2. Grease a 9x13-inch baking dish.
3. Cook the lasagna noodles according to package instructions.
4. Drain, then rinse with cold water.
5. Heat the olive oil over medium heat in a skillet.
6. Add the onion and garlic and cook until the onion is tender, stirring occasionally.
7. Stir in the spinach, ricotta, Parmesan, salt, pepper and nutmeg.
8. Heat through.
9. In the prepared baking dish, place a layer of noodles, spread half the spinach mixture over the noodles, then sprinkle with 1 cup of the mozzarella cheese.
10. Make another layer of noodles and top with the remaining spinach mixture and mozzarella cheese.
11. Top with a final layer of noodles.
12. Cover the baking dish with foil and bake for 40 minutes.
13. Remove foil and bake 15 minutes longer, or until cheese is bubbly and starts to brown.

Nutrition Information:
Calories: 270, Fat: 16 g, Saturated fat: 8 g, Cholesterol: 37 mg, Sodium: 653 mg, Carbohydrate: 17 g, Fiber: 2 g, Protein: 15 g.

5. Mushroom Ragout with Fettuccine

Mushroom Ragout with Fettuccine is a savory Italian dish made with a creamy parmesan sauce, mushrooms, and delicious fettuccine noodles. This rustic Italian meal is sure to be a hit for a cozy night in.

Serving: 4
| Preparation Time: 15 minutes
| Ready Time: 20 minutes

Ingredients:
-1 lb. fresh fettuccine noodles
-3 cloves garlic, minced
-2 tablespoons olive oil
-2 cups mushrooms (any variety)
-1/2 cup dry white wine
-2 tablespoons butter
-1 teaspoon Italian seasoning
-1 cup cream
-1 cup parmesan cheese, grated
-Salt and pepper to taste

Instructions:
1. Bring a large pot of salted water to a boil. Cook fettuccine noodles according to package instructions, drain and set aside.
2. Heat a large skillet over medium-high heat. Add olive oil and garlic and sauté for 1 minute.
3. Add mushrooms and sauté for 3 minutes until lightly browned.
4. Add wine and simmer for 3 minutes until most of the wine has evaporated.
5. Reduce heat to low and add butter, Italian seasoning, cream, and parmesan cheese. Simmer for 5 minutes until sauce has thickened.
6. Add cooked fettuccine noodles to sauce and gently toss to combine.
7. Season with salt and pepper to taste.

Nutrition Information:
Calories: 425 calories per serving;
Total Fat: 16 grams;
Saturated Fat: 9 grams;
Cholesterol: 43 milligrams;
Sodium: 400 milligrams;
Total Carbohydrate: 43 grams;
Protein: 17 grams.

6. Cheesy Broccoli Soup

An indulgent, cheesy delight, this creamy Broccoli Soup is sure to become a family favorite! It's vegan-adaptable and full of delicious, comforting flavors.

Serves 4 - 6. | Preparation Time: 10 minutes. | Ready Time: 25 minutes.

Ingredients:
- 2 tablespoons olive oil
- 2 large sweet onions, chopped
- 4 cloves garlic, minced
- 4 cups vegetable stock
- 2 large heads of broccoli, chopped
- 1 cup vegan cream cheese or heavy cream
- 1 1/2 cups shredded vegan cheese or regular cheese
- 2 tablespoons nutritional yeast
- 2 tablespoons freshly green herbs, for garnish

Instructions:
1. Heat the olive oil in a large pot over medium heat. Add the onions and cook, stirring occasionally, until the onions begin to soften, about 5 minutes.
2. Add the garlic and cook, stirring often, until the garlic is fragrant, about 1 minute.
3. Add the vegetable stock, broccoli and vegan cream cheese, cover the pot and bring the mixture to a boil. Reduce the heat and simmer until the broccoli is cooked through, about 10 minutes.
4. Remove the pot from the heat and stir in the vegan cheese and nutritional yeast until it is completely melted.
5. Transfer the soup to a food processor and blend the soup until it is creamy and smooth.
6. Transfer the soup back to the pot, over medium heat, and cook until the soup is hot and thickened, about 8 minutes.
7. Serve the soup topped with a sprinkle of freshly chopped herbs.

Nutrition Information:
Calories: 303, Total Fat: 17 g, Saturated Fat: 7 g, Sodium: 819 mg, Carbohydrates: 23 g, Fiber: 6 g, Sugar: 8 g, Protein: 13 g

Love the fulfilling taste of savory zucchini? Satisfy cravings with this easy-to-make zucchini fritter recipe. Made with zucchini, garlic, Parmesan cheese, and stuffed with a creamy ricotta filling, these fritters look amazing and taste even better.

Serving: 4
| Preparation Time: 10 minutes
| Ready Time: 18 minutes

Ingredients:
- 2 medium-sized zucchinis, grated
- 1/4 cup all-purpose flour
- 2 cloves of garlic, minced
- 2 tablespoons of grated Parmesan cheese
- Salt and pepper, to taste
- 1/2 cup ricotta cheese
- 2 eggs, whisked
- Vegetable oil, for frying

Instructions:
1. Using cheesecloth, squeeze as much of the moisture out of the grated zucchini as possible.
2. In a large bowl, combine the zucchini, flour, garlic, Parmesan cheese, and season with salt and pepper.
3. In a medium bowl, mix together the ricotta cheese and eggs.
4. Form the zucchini mixture into small patties and carefully stuff each one with about a tablespoon of ricotta cheese mixture.
5. In a large skillet over medium-high heat, heat the vegetable oil. Once the oil is hot, add the fritters and cook until golden brown, flipping once during cooking, about 5 minutes per side.

Nutrition Information (per serving):
Calories: 279, Total Fat: 20, Cholesterol: 86, Sodium: 254, Total Carbohydrates: 14, Dietary Fiber: 3, Sugars: 5, Protein: 11

8. Potato Gnocchi with Creamy Garlic Sauce

Potato Gnocchi with Creamy Garlic Sauce is a savory and flavorful Italian dish made from pillowy-soft potato dumplings and a delicious garlic cream sauce. This creamy, comforting dinner is the perfect way to use up leftover potatoes and will make for a delightful evening meal.
Serving: 4 servings
| Preparation Time: 15 minutes
| Ready Time: 25 minutes

Ingredients:
-3 cups mashed potatoes
-2 large eggs
-1 cup all-purpose flour, plus more for dusting
-1/4 teaspoon kosher salt
-1/2 cup butter
-4 cloves garlic, minced
-1 cup heavy cream
-2 tablespoons freshly chopped parsley
-1 teaspoon freshly cracked black pepper
-Grated Parmesan cheese, for serving (optional)

Instructions:
1. In a large bowl, combine the mashed potatoes and eggs until fully combined. Gradually add in the flour and salt and knead until a cohesive dough forms.
2. Divide the dough into 4 equal pieces. Roll each piece out into a 12-inch-long rope on a lightly floured surface.
3. Cut each rope into 1-inch pieces and lightly roll each piece against the back of a fork to create Gnocchi. Place on a baking sheet lined with parchment paper.
4. In a large skillet over medium heat, melt the butter. Add the garlic and cook until fragrant, about 2 minutes.
5. Add the cream and parsley and bring to a simmer. Add the Gnocchi to the pan and season with the black pepper. Stir to combine and cook until the Gnocchi are tender, about 5 minutes.
6. Divide the Gnocchi among 4 plates and top with Parmesan cheese, if desired. Serve immediately.

Nutrition Information:
Calories: 426, Fat: 28g, Saturated Fat: 18g, Cholesterol: 148mg, Sodium: 718mg, Carbohydrates: 30g, Fiber: 2g, Sugar: 2g, Protein:10g

9. Macaroni and Cheese with Bacon

Macaroni and Cheese with Bacon is an indulgent comfort food with a delicious salty, smoky twist. This easy recipe takes only 25 minutes to prepare and can serve up to 8 people. It is sure to please the entire family and make a great weeknight meal.

Serving: 8
| Preparation Time: 10 minutes
| Ready Time: 15 minutes

Ingredients:
- 1 lb macaroni noodles
- 4 cups sharp cheddar cheese, shredded
- 4 cups whole milk
- 4 tbsp butter
- 4 tbsp all-purpose flour
- 2 tsp mustard powder
- 1/4 tsp nutmeg
- 2 cloves garlic, minced
- 2 cups cooked bacon, chopped
- Salt and pepper to taste

Instructions:
1. Preheat oven to 375F (190C).
2. Bring a large pot of salted water to a boil. Add the macaroni and cook according to instructions on the package. Drain and set aside.
3. In a large saucepan, melt the butter over medium heat. Add the garlic and cook until fragrant.
4. Whisk in the flour and cook for 1-2 minutes.
5. Slowly stir in the milk, adding a little at a time. Simmer for 5 minutes, stirring occasionally.
6. Add the mustard powder, nutmeg, salt and pepper. Whisk until combined.
7. Remove from heat and add in the cheese. Stir until melted.
8. In a large bowl, combine the cheese sauce, cooked macaroni, bacon and stir together until combined.

9. Grease a 9x13 baking dish with butter. Pour the macaroni and cheese mixture into the dish and spread around to cover the bottom.
10. Bake for 15 minutes. Let cool for 5 minutes before serving.

Nutrition Information:
Calories: 493 kcal, Protein: 21 g, Carbohydrates: 46 g, Fat: 22 g, Saturated Fat: 12 g, Cholesterol: 59 mg, Sodium: 632 mg, Fiber: 2 g, Sugar: 7 g

10. French Onion Soup

French Onion Soup is a classic and comforting French dish with sweet caramelized onions in a savory beef broth. Serve this delicious soup with a side of crunchy croutons or a slice of toasted baguette for a flavorful meal.
Serving: 4-6
| Preparation Time: 35 minutes
| Ready Time: 50 minutes

Ingredients:
- olive oil
- 4 medium sweet onions, sliced
- 4 cloves garlic, minced
- 2 tablespoons butter
- 8 cups beef stock
- 2 tablespoons all-purpose flour
- 2 bay leaves
- 2 tablespoons Worcestershire sauce
- 1/2 cup dry red wine
- 2 tablespoons fresh thyme
- 1 tablespoon chopped fresh parsley
- Salt and freshly ground black pepper, to taste

Instructions:
1. Heat the olive oil in a large skillet over medium-high heat. Add the onions and garlic and cook, stirring frequently, until the onions are golden brown, about 10 minutes. Add the butter and stir for a few minutes.

2. Add the stock, flour, bay leaves, Worcestershire sauce, and red wine and bring to a boil. Reduce the heat and simmer for 30 minutes. Remove the bay leaves.

3. Add the thyme and parsley and season with salt and pepper. Simmer for 5 minutes more, or until the soup is heated through. Serve.

Nutrition Information:
Serving size: 1/6 of recipe (about 1 cup)
Calories: 109
Fat: 2 grams
Carbohydrates: 11 grams
Protein: 7 grams
Sodium: 510 mg

11. Eggplant Parmesan

Eggplant Parmesan is an Italian classic comfort food. It's a delicious vegetarian dish that is made with layers of eggplant, topped with tomato sauce and cheese. This recipe is sure to satisfy even the pickiest of eaters.
Serving: 4
| Preparation Time: 20 minutes

Ingredients:
- 2 large eggplant, thinly sliced
- 2 cups tomato sauce
- 2 teaspoon oregano
- 2 teaspoon parsley
- 1 cup grated Parmesan
- 1/2 cup vegetable oil
- Salt and pepper to taste

Instructions:
1. Preheat oven to 350F.
2. Slice eggplant into thin slices and salt lightly.
3. Heat oil in a large shallow skillet.
4. Fry the eggplant slices in the oil until golden brown on both sides.
5. Layer half of the eggplant slices over the bottom of an 11x7-inch baking dish.

6. Spoon half of the tomato sauce over the eggplant slices.
7. Sprinkle half of the oregano, parsley, parmesan, and salt and pepper over the tomato sauce.
8. Repeat steps 5-7.
9. Cover baking dish with foil and bake for 45 minutes.
10. If desired, you can broil for the last 5 minutes to brown the top layer of cheese.

Nutrition Information:
Calories: 290; Fat: 18.2g; Carbohydrates: 21.2g; Protein: 11g; Fiber: 8.5g.

12. Beef Stroganoff

Beef Stroganoff is a hearty and delicious dish that combines tender pieces of beef, mushrooms and sour cream all in a flavorful sauce. It's sure to be a hit with your family and friends.
Serving: Serves 4-6
| Preparation Time: 15 minutes
| Ready Time: 35 minutes

Ingredients:
1. 1 lb beef cut into thin strips
2. 1/2 cup all-purpose flour
3. 2 onions, finely chopped
4. 3 cloves garlic, chopped
5. 8 ounces of mushrooms, sliced
6. 1/2 teaspoon dried thyme
7. 2 tablespoons butter
8. 3 tablespoons tomato paste
9. 3 tablespoons Worcestershire sauce
10. 1/4 cup dry white wine
11. 1 cup beef stock
12. 1/2 cup sour cream
13. Salt and freshly ground pepper to taste

Instructions:
1. Place the beef strips in a bowl and season with salt and pepper. Toss in the flour to coat.

2. Heat the butter in a large pan over medium heat. Add the beef strips and cook until golden brown, about 4 minutes.

3. Add the onion, garlic, mushrooms and thyme and cook until the onion is softened, about 5 minutes.

4. Add the tomato paste, Worcestershire sauce and white wine and cook for a few more minutes.

5. Add the beef stock and bring the mixture to a boil, then reduce the heat and let simmer for about 20 minutes or until the beef is tender.

6. Add the sour cream and cook for a few minutes to heat through.

7. Serve over egg noodles or with rice.

Nutrition Information:
Calories: 317 | Fat: 13 g | Carbs: 19 g | Protein: 26 g

13. Baked Ziti

Baked Ziti is an Italian-American dish made of ziti pasta, a creamy tomato sauce, and melted cheese. Served hot and hearty, it's a guaranteed crowd-pleaser!
Serving: 8-10
| Preparation Time: 20 minutes
| Ready Time: 50 minutes

Ingredients:
1. 1 lb. Ziti pasta
2. 2 jars/cans of tomato/marinara sauce
3. 2 cups low-fat ricotta cheese
4. 2 tsps oregano
5. 1 cup grated Parmesan cheese
6. 4 cups grated mozzarella cheese

Instructions:
1. Preheat the oven to 350F degrees.

2. Bring a large pot of salted water to a boil. Boil the ziti for 8 minutes, then drain and set aside.

3. In a large bowl, mix together the ricotta cheese, oregano, half of the Parmesan cheese, and half of the mozzarella cheese.

4. Grease a 9x13-inch baking dish and spread 1/2 cup of the tomato sauce over the bottom of the pan.

5. Layer the ziti in the baking dish, followed by the ricotta mixture. Pour 1 1/2 cups of the tomato sauce and spread over the cheese.

6. Top with the remaining Parmesan cheese and mozzarella cheese.

7. Bake uncovered for 30-40 minutes, or until the cheese is bubbly and golden.

Nutrition Information:
Calories: 531
Total Fat: 18g
Saturated Fat: 9g
Cholesterol: 49mg
Sodium: 750mg
Carbohydrates: 60g
Protein: 28g

14. Tomato and Basil Soup

Tomato and Basil Soup is a classic and comforting meal perfect for a warm and cozy night. This flavorful soup is made with simple ingredients and can be ready in under 30 minutes!
Serving 6
| Preparation Time: 10 minutes
| Ready Time: 30 minutes

Ingredients
- 2 tablespoons olive oil
- 2 cloves garlic, minced
- 1/2 onion, diced
- 4 cups chicken broth
- 2 (14-ounce) cans fire-roasted diced tomatoes
- 1/2 cup fresh basil, chopped
- 1/2 teaspoon dried oregano
- Salt and pepper to taste

Instructions
1. Heat olive oil in a large pot over medium heat.

2. Add garlic and onion, and sauté for about 2 minutes.
3. Add chicken broth, tomatoes, basil, oregano and salt and pepper.
Bring to a boil, then reduce heat and simmer for 15 minutes.
4. Puree the soup with an immersion blender until smooth.
5. Serve hot with crusty bread or croutons.

Nutrition Information
Serving size: 1 cup
Calories: 100
Fat: 5g
Carbohydrates: 10g
Protein: 3g

15. Summer Vegetable Risotto

Summer Vegetable Risotto is a quick and zesty dish that is perfect for the
summer months. This risotto is loaded with delicious summer
ingredients like zucchini, corn, and cherry tomatoes and cooked in a light
and flavorful broth.
Serving: 4-6
| Preparation Time: 25 minutes
| Ready Time: 30-35 minutes

Ingredients:
1. 2 tablespoons olive oil
2. 1/2 cup diced onion
3. 2 cloves garlic, minced
4. 2 cups arborio rice
5. 5 cups vegetable broth
6. 1 cup freshly grated Parmesan cheese
7. 1 cup fresh or frozen corn
8. 1 cup diced zucchini
9. 1 cup cherry tomatoes, halved
10. Salt and pepper to taste

Instructions:

1. Heat the olive oil in a large saucepan over medium heat. Add the onions and garlic and cook for 3-4 minutes, stirring occasionally, until the onions are softened.
2. Add the arborio rice and stir to coat in the onion/garlic mixture. Pour in the vegetable broth and bring to a boil. Reduce the heat to low, cover, and simmer for 20 minutes, stirring occasionally.
3. Add the Parmesan, corn, zucchini, and tomatoes and stir to combine. Cover and cook for an additional 5-10 minutes, until the vegetables are tender and the risotto is creamy.
4. Adjust the seasoning with salt and pepper as desired and serve.

Nutrition Information:
Per serving (1/4 of recipe): calories: 383; fat: 9g; carbs: 60g; protein: 12g

16. Cauliflower and Potato Curry

Cauliflower and Potato Curry is a flavorful and aromatic dish that is perfect for a weeknight dinner. It has the perfect mix of spices and vegetables, and is just as delicious as it is nutritious.
Serving: yields 4-5 servings
| Preparation Time: 15 minutes
| Ready Time:1 hour

Ingredients:
- 2 tablespoons olive oil
-1 onion, chopped
-3 cloves garlic, minced
-1 teaspoon cumin powder
-1 teaspoon turmeric powder
-2 teaspoons coriander powder
-1 inch piece of ginger, grated or minced
-1 can of diced tomatoes
-2 medium potatoes, cubed
-1 large head cauliflower, cut into florets
-1 can of coconut milk
-salt and pepper to taste
-fresh cilantro for garnish

Instructions:
1. Heat the olive oil in a large pot over medium-high heat. Add the onion and sauté until softened, about 5 minutes.
2. Add the garlic, cumin, turmeric, coriander, and ginger and sauté for another minute.
3. Add the diced tomatoes, potatoes, and cauliflower and mix to coat in the spices.
4. Pour in the coconut milk, season with salt and pepper, and bring to a low simmer.
5. Cook for about 30 minutes, until the potatoes and cauliflower are tender.
6. Garnish with fresh cilantro and serve hot.

Nutrition Information:
Per serving: Calories 290, Fat 16g, Saturated Fat 11g, Trans Fat 0g, Carbohydrates 31g, Fiber 8g, Total Sugars 6g, Protein 7g, Sodium 130mg, Cholesterol 0mg.

17. Carrot and Parsnip Soup

Carrot and parsnip soup is a delicious and nutritious winter soup. Rich in healthy carbohydrates, vitamins A and C, and potassium, this recipe is sure to be a hit for the entire family.
Serving: Serves 4.
| Preparation Time: 20 minutes
| Ready Time: 40 minutes

Ingredients:
- 4 parsnips, chopped
- 2 tablespoons olive oil
- 1 onion, diced
- 2 cloves garlic, minced
- 4 carrots, chopped
- 2 cups vegetable broth
- 1 teaspoon dried thyme
- Salt and pepper to taste

Instructions:

1. Heat the olive oil in a large pot over medium heat.
2. Add the diced onion and garlic, and cook for 3 minutes, stirring occasionally.
3. Add the parsnips and carrots, and cook for another 5 minutes, stirring occasionally.
4. Pour in the vegetable broth, and stir in the thyme, salt, and pepper.
5. Bring to a boil, reduce to a simmer, and let cook for 30 minutes, stirring occasionally.
6. Use an immersion blender (or transfer to a standing blender in batches) to blend the soup until smooth.
7. Serve warm with crusty bread or a green salad.

Nutrition Information:
Calories: 121, Fat: 5.7g, Carbohydrates: 16.1g, Protein: 2.2g, Cholesterol: 0mg, Sodium: 533mg, Fiber: 4.4g, Potassium: 501.4 mg.

18. Red Lentil Dal

Red Lentil Dal is an easy and nutritious savory dish that is perfect for a comforting weeknight meal. This vegan Indian dal is hearty and flavorful from warming spices and made with red lentils, tomatoes, and fragrant garlic and ginger.
Serving: 6
| Preparation Time: 10 minutes
| Ready Time: 25 minutes

Ingredients:
- 2 tablespoons vegetable oil
- 1 onion, diced
- 2 cloves garlic, minced
- 1 teaspoon ginger, grated
- 2 teaspoons ground cumin
- 1 teaspoon ground turmeric
- 1 teaspoon ground coriander
- 1 teaspoon dry red chili flakes (optional)
- 1 (29 oz) can diced tomatoes
- 2 cups red lentils
- 4 cups vegetable broth

- salt and pepper, to taste

Instructions:
1. Heat oil in a large pot over medium-high heat. Add the onion and cook until softened, about 3-4 minutes.
2. Add garlic, ginger, cumin, turmeric, red chili flakes and stir for about 1 minute.
3. Add diced tomatoes to the pot and bring to a boil. Once boiling, add the lentils and vegetable broth and mix well.
4. Lower the heat and simmer the dal until lentils are tender and the sauce has thickened, about 15-20 minutes. Season with salt and pepper.

Nutrition Information (per serving):
262 calories; 7.2 g fat; 10 g saturated fat; 0 mg cholesterol; 997 mg sodium; 33 g carbohydrates; 6.8 g dietary fiber; 9.3 g sugar; 14.3 g protein.

19. Spinach and Mushroom Quiche

This savory Spinach and Mushroom Quiche is a simple and delicious dish to make for any meal or gathering. It's full of flavor and nutrition and so easy to make - all you need is a few ingredients and some simple instructions.
Serving: 8
| Preparation Time: 10 minutes
| Ready Time: 40 minutes

Ingredients:
- 2 tablespoons of olive oil
- 2 cloves of garlic, minced
- 1 small onion, diced
- 2 cups mushrooms, thinly sliced
- 250 grams of baby spinach
- 4 eggs
- 1 cup heavy cream
- 1/2 teaspoon of salt and pepper
- 1/3 cup shredded cheese
- 1 (9 inch) store-bought frozen pie crust

Instructions:

1. Preheat oven to 350F (180C).
2. Heat olive oil in a large skillet over medium heat. Add garlic, onion, and mushrooms and cook for 5 minutes.
3. Add baby spinach and cook for a few more minutes until tender.
4. In a large bowl, whisk together eggs, cream, salt and pepper.
5. Place the pie crust in a 9 inch baking dish, and pour the egg mixture over it.
6. Top with cooked vegetables and sprinkle the top with cheese.
7. Bake in preheated oven for 30 minutes.

Nutrition Information:

per serving: 273 calories, 19.5 g fat, 10.3 g carbohydrates, 2.8 g protein

20. Greek-Style Orzo Salad

Greek-Style Orzo Salad is an incredibly flavorful, yet simple dish that is sure to be a crowd favorite! With just a handful of ingredients, this orzo salad is rapidly prepared and makes for a great side or main dish.
Serving: 6
| Preparation Time: 10 minutes
| Ready Time: 15 minutes

Ingredients:

1. 4 cups cooked orzo
2. 1/4 cup feta cheese, crumbled
3. 1/4 cup kalamata olives, pitted and roughly chopped
4. 4 scallions, white and light green parts, chopped
5. 1 14-ounce can artichoke hearts, drained and chopped
6. 1/4 cup extra-virgin olive oil
7. 2 tablespoons fresh lemon juice
8. 2 tablespoons fresh oregano, chopped
9. Kosher salt and freshly ground black pepper, to taste

Instructions:

1. In a large bowl, combine the cooked orzo, feta cheese, olives, scallions and artichoke hearts.

2. In a small bowl, whisk together the olive oil, lemon juice and oregano until blended.
3. Pour the dressing over the orzo mixture and stir until everything is evenly coated.
4. Season to taste with salt and pepper.

Nutrition Information (per serving):
Calories: 224, Fat: 11.6g, Saturated Fat: 2.5g, Cholesterol: 8mg, Sodium: 299mg, Carbohydrates: 23.7g, Fiber: 2.6g, Sugar: 0.2g, Protein: 5.1g

21. Beef and Bean Chili

Beef and Bean Chili is a hearty, flavorful weeknight dish that is so simple to make. An easy combination of ground beef, canned beans, and tomato-based ingredients, this chili makes for a filling yet healthy meal. Serve with rice, cornbread, or warm tortillas for a full meal.
Serving: Makes 8 servings
| Preparation Time: 15 minutes
| Ready Time: 40 minutes

Ingredients:
- 1 pound lean ground beef
- 1 small onion, diced
- 2 cloves garlic, minced
- 1 teaspoon chile powder
- 1 teaspoon cumin
- 2 cans (14.5-ounce) diced tomatoes
- 2 cans (15-ounce) black beans, drained and rinsed
- 1 can (15.25-ounce) corn, drained
- 2 cups low-sodium beef broth
- 1 teaspoon smoked paprika
- 1 teaspoon dried oregano
- Salt and freshly ground black pepper, to taste

Instructions:
1. Heat a large Dutch oven over medium heat. Add the ground beef and onion and cook until the beef is no longer pink, stirring often to break up the meat.

2. Add the garlic, chile powder, and cumin, and cook for about 1 minute to bloom the spices.

3. Add the tomatoes, black beans, corn, beef broth, and smoked paprika, and bring to a simmer.

4. Reduce the heat to low and simmer uncovered for 20 minutes, stirring occasionally.

5. Add the oregano and season with salt and pepper to taste. Simmer for another 5 to 10 minutes, until the chili has thickened.

Nutrition Information:
Per serving: 220 calories, 5.5g fat, 26g carbohydrates, 12g protein

22. Broccoli and Cheddar Soup

This creamy Broccoli and Cheddar Soup makes for a warm and hearty meal. It is made with fresh broccoli, sharp cheddar cheese, vegetable broth, and cream cheese then cooked until tender.
Serving: 4 servings
| Preparation Time: 10 minutes
| Ready Time: 45 minutes

Ingredients:
- 2 tablespoons butter
- 1 small onion, diced
- 2 cloves garlic, minced
- 2 cups vegetable broth
- 2 1/2 cups milk
- 2 heads of fresh broccoli, chopped
- 8 ounces sharp cheddar cheese, shredded
- 1/3 cup cream cheese
- Salt and pepper to taste

Instructions:
1. Heat butter in a large pot over medium-high heat.
2. Add the onion and garlic, sautéing until softened, about 5 minutes.
3. Pour in the vegetable broth and milk, and bring to a low boil.
4. Add the broccoli and reduce heat to low-medium. Simmer for 20 minutes, or until the broccoli is very tender.

5. Remove the pot from heat and stir in the cheddar and cream cheese until melted.

6. Using a blender or immersion blender, puree the soup until it reaches desired texture.

7. Adjust seasoning with salt and pepper to taste.

Nutrition Information:
Calories: 258, Fat: 18g, Carbohydrates: 13g, Protein: 14g, Cholesterol: 53mg, Sodium: 577mg, Fiber: 3.2g

23. Chicken and Rice Casserole

Chicken and Rice Casserole is a classic comfort food dish that is sure to please the whole family. A combination of creamy chicken, vegetables and rice baked together, this casserole is warming, delicious, and simple to make. Serve with a green salad to complete the meal.

Serving: 6-8
| Preparation Time: 15 minutes
| Ready Time: 1 hour

Ingredients:
- 1 1/2 cups long-grain white rice
- 2 tablespoons olive oil
- 1 onion, diced
- 1 bell pepper, diced
- 3 cloves garlic, minced
- 2 cups cooked chicken, diced
- 1 can diced tomatoes, drained
- 1 can cream of chicken soup
- 1/2 cup heavy cream
- 2 1/2 cups shredded cheddar cheese
- Salt and pepper, to taste

Instructions:
1. Preheat oven to 375F (190°C).
2. In a large pot, cook the rice according to package instructions.
3. Heat the olive oil in a large skillet over medium heat. Add the onion, bell pepper, and garlic and cook until softened.

4. Stir in the cooked chicken, diced tomatoes, and cream of chicken soup. Simmer for 3-5 minutes.

5. Stir in the cooked rice, heavy cream, and 1 cup of the cheddar cheese. Season with salt and pepper.

6. Transfer to a 9x13 inch baking dish. Top with remaining cheese.

7. Bake for 20 minutes, or until cheese is melted and the casserole is hot and bubbly.

Nutrition Information:
Calories: 319 kcal, Carbohydrates: 26 g, Protein: 17 g, Fat: 14 g, Saturated Fat: 7 g, Cholesterol: 49 mg, Sodium: 517 mg, Potassium: 306 mg, Fiber: 1 g, Sugar: 1 g, Vitamin A: 595 IU, Vitamin C: 27 mg, Calcium: 189 mg, Iron: 1 mg.

24. Zucchini Lasagna

Zucchini Lasagna is a delicious, vegetarian-friendly dinner that's sure to please the whole family. This layered dish substitutes zucchini for lasagna noodles and is filled with savory, cheesy ricotta filling, marinara sauce, and a sprinkle of fresh herbs.

Serving: 8-10
| Preparation Time: 20 minutes
| Ready Time: 45 minutes

Ingredients:
- 3-4 medium zucchinis
- 1/2 cup ricotta cheese
- 1/2 cup grated parmesan cheese
- 1/4 cup chopped fresh herbs (parsley, basil, oregano)
- 2 cups marinara sauce
- 8 ounces grated mozzarella cheese
- salt and pepper to taste

Instructions:
1. Preheat oven to 350 degrees F (175 degrees C).
2. Slice the zucchini into thin slices, about 1/4-1/2 inch thick.
3. In a bowl, combine the ricotta, parmesan, herbs, and salt and pepper.

4. In a 9x13 inch baking dish spread a thin layer of marinara sauce on the bottom, and cover with a layer of zucchini slices.
5. Spread half of the ricotta mixture over the zucchini.
6. Spread another thin layer of marinara sauce on top, and then sprinkle with half of the mozzarella cheese.
7. Layer another layer of zucchini and repeat step 5.
8. Top with a layer of mozzarella cheese.
9. Bake for 30-35 minutes or until cheese is melted and bubbly.

Nutrition Information:
Calories: 211, Fat: 13.2g, Saturated Fat: 6.2g, Cholesterol: 27mg, Sodium: 369mg, Carbohydrates: 11.3g, Fiber: 2.3g, Sugar: 4.6g, Protein: 11.2g.

25. Stuffed Peppers with Rice and Ground Beef

Stuffed Peppers with Rice and Ground Beef is a delicious and comforting dish that your whole family will love. Combining protein-packed beef, tender peppers, and fluffy rice, this easy recipe is sure to satisfy.
Servings: 4
| Preparation Time: 15 minutes
| Ready Time: 40 minutes

Ingredients:
- 4 bell peppers, any color, cored and seeded
- 1 tablespoon olive oil
- 1 small onion, chopped
- 1 lb. ground beef
- 2 cloves garlic, minced
- 1 teaspoon dried oregano
- 1 teaspoon ground cumin
- 1 cup cooked white or basmati rice
- 1 (14.5-ounce) can diced tomatoes
- 1 cup shredded cheddar cheese

Instructions:
1. Preheat oven to 350F.
2. Place peppers in a 9 x13-inch baking dish.

3. Heat oil in a large skillet over medium-high heat. Add onion and cook for 3 to 4 minutes, stirring occasionally.

4. Add ground beef, garlic, oregano and cumin, and cook for 7 to 10 minutes, breaking it apart with a spoon, until the meat is browned.

5. Remove from heat and stir in the cooked rice, diced tomatoes, and half of the cheese.

6. Spoon this mixture into the prepared peppers, and top with the remaining cheese.

7. Bake in the preheated oven for 25 minutes, until the peppers are tender and the cheese is melted.

Nutrition Information:
Calories: 428 calories
Fat: 20 g
Carbohydrates: 34 g
Protein: 25 g
Sodium: 555 mg
Potassium: 920 mg
Fiber: 4 g
Sugar: 4 g
Vitamin A: 1207IU
Vitamin C: 128 mg
Calcium: 182 mg
Iron: 3.5 mg

26. Pork Fried Rice

Pork Fried Rice is a classic Chinese dish with a zesty garlic and ginger flavor, and just the right amount of crunch. It is quick and easy to make, and is sure to be a hit with the whole family.
Serving: 4
| Preparation Time: 10 minutes
| Ready Time: 15 minutes

Ingredients:
1. 2 cups cooked white rice, cooled
2. 4 tablespoons vegetable oil, divided
3. 1 pound pork loin, cubed

4. 2 garlic cloves, minced
5. 1 teaspoon grated ginger
6. 1 medium onion, chopped
7. 1 red bell pepper, chopped
8. 2 carrots, chopped
9. 2 green onions, diced
10. 2 tablespoons reduced-sodium soy sauce
11. 1 tablespoons rice vinegar
12. 1/4 teaspoon white pepper

Instructions:
1. Heat 2 tablespoons of the oil in a large skillet over medium-high heat.
2. Add the pork cubes, garlic, and ginger and cook until the pork is lightly browned and just cooked through, about 5 minutes.
3. Add the onion, bell pepper, carrots, and green onions, and cook for 2 minutes.
4. Push the pork and vegetables to the sides of the pan and add the remaining 2 tablespoons of oil in the middle.
5. Add the cooled cooked rice and cook for 2 minutes.
6. Pour the soy sauce, rice vinegar, and white pepper over the top, then stir to combine.
7. Cook until the rice is hot and lightly browned, about 3 to 5 minutes.

Nutrition Information:
Serving Size: 1/4 of recipe
Calories: 391
Total Fat: 20 g
Saturated Fat: 3 g
Cholesterol: 39 mg
Sodium: 483 mg
Total Carbohydrate: 36 g
Dietary Fiber: 2 g
Protein: 16 g

27. Creamy Mushroom Tagliatelle

Creamy Mushroom Tagliatelle is an indulgent, yet simple dish that requires minimal ingredients and has a deliciously rich flavor. It is a great way to treat yourself for a weeknight dinner.

Serving: 4
| Preparation Time: 10 minutes
| Ready in: 25 minutes

Ingredients:
- 10-12 mushrooms (sliced)
- 1/2 onion (chopped)
- 2 cloves garlic (minced)
- 1/4 cup white wine
- 1 tablespoon cornstarch
- 2 tablespoons butter
- 1/4 cup half and half
- 1 1/2 cups chicken broth
- 1 teaspoon Italian seasoning
- 1 teaspoon fresh parsley (chopped)
- 1/2 teaspoon black pepper
- 250g tagliatelle
- 1/4 cup Parmesan cheese (grated)

Instructions:
1. Bring a large pot of salted water to a boil, and add the tagliatelle. Cook until al dente, according to package instructions. Drain and set aside.
2. Meanwhile, melt the butter in a large skillet. Add the onion and mushrooms and cook for 3 minutes.
3. Add the garlic and cook for one minute more.
4. In a small bowl, whisk together the white wine and cornstarch.
5. Add to the skillet, followed by the chicken broth, half and half, Italian seasoning, parsley, and black pepper.
6. Bring to a boil, reduce heat, and simmer for 4-5 minutes, until sauce has thickened.
7. Add the cooked tagliatelle to the skillet and toss to combine with the sauce.
8. Sprinkle the Parmesan cheese, and serve.

Nutrition Information:
Calories: 267 kcal, Carbohydrates: 33 g, Protein: 7 g, Fat: 10 g, Saturated Fat: 5 g, Cholesterol: 24 mg, Sodium: 511 mg, Potassium: 205 mg, Fiber:

2 g, Sugar: 3 g, Vitamin A: 271 IU, Vitamin C: 4 mg, Calcium: 74 mg, Iron: 1 mg

28. Butternut Squash Soup

Butternut Squash Soup is a delicious, hearty, and healthy fall soup, made with squash and creamy coconut milk.
Serving: 4
| Preparation Time: 15 minutes
| Ready Time: 40 minutes

Ingredients:
• 2 tablespoons olive oil
• 1 bunch scallions, sliced
• 2 cloves garlic, minced
• 2 teaspoons curry powder
• 4 cups peeled and cubed butternut squash
• 2 cups vegetable broth
• 1 can (14oz) full-fat coconut milk
• 2 tablespoons maple syrup
• 1 teaspoon sea salt
• Freshly ground black pepper

Instructions:
1. Heat the olive oil in a large soup pot over medium heat.
2. Add the scallions, garlic and curry powder and cook for about 5 minutes until the scallions begin to soften.
3. Add the squash, broth, coconut milk, maple syrup, and salt and bring to a simmer.
4. Reduce the heat to low, cover and simmer for 25 minutes, or until the squash is tender.
5. Use an immersion blender to puree the soup until smooth.
6. Add freshly ground black pepper to taste.

Nutrition Information:
Per serving: 207 Calories, 15g Fat, 11g Carbohydrates, 2g Protein, 2g Fiber.

29. Turkey Meatloaf

A classic and flavorful dish, Turkey Meatloaf is an easy and delicious choice for weeknight dinners. This family favorite features ground turkey, hearty oats, flavorful seasonings, and a simple glaze for topping. It has a delicious combination of flavors that will please the whole family.

Serving: 8
| Preparation Time: 25 minutes
| Ready Time: 1 hour

Ingredients:
- 1 tablespoon olive oil
- 1 small onion, diced
- 2 cloves garlic, minced
- 1 1/2 pounds ground turkey
- 1/2 cup rolled oats
- 2 tablespoons Worcestershire sauce
- 1/4 cup ketchup, divided
- 2 teaspoons Italian seasoning
- 1 teaspoon garlic powder
- 1/2 teaspoon dried oregano
- 1/2 teaspoon onion powder
- 1/2 teaspoon salt
- 1/4 teaspoon black pepper
- 2 large eggs

Instructions:
1. Preheat oven to 375F. Grease a 9x5-inch loaf pan with cooking spray.
2. Heat olive oil in a skillet over medium-high heat. Add onion and garlic and cook until lightly browned, about 5 minutes.
3. In a large bowl, combine ground turkey, oats, Worcestershire sauce, 2 tablespoons ketchup, Italian seasoning, garlic powder, oregano, onion powder, salt, pepper, eggs, and cooked onion and garlic. Mix with hands until combined.
4. Transfer mixture to prepared loaf pan and press down into the pan to fill it evenly. Spread remaining 2 tablespoons ketchup on top of the loaf.

5. Bake in preheated oven for 40-45 minutes, or until the internal temperature of the meatloaf reaches 165F.
6. Let cool for 10 minutes before slicing and serving.

Nutrition Information:
-Calories: 224.2
-Total Fat: 10.6g
-Saturated Fat: 2.7g
-Cholesterol: 130.1mg
-Sodium: 343.9mg
-Carbohydrates: 9.3g
-Fiber: 1.3g
-Sugar: 1.9g
-Protein: 22.7g

30. Hummus

Hummus is a versatile, healthy, and delicious Middle Eastern dip and spread. It is simple to make and uses ingredients that can easily be found in any supermarket.
Serving 4-6, | Preparation Time 10 minutes, ready time 10 minutes.

Ingredients:
1. 2 tablespoons extra-virgin olive oil;
2. Two 15 -ounce cans chickpeas, drained and rinsed;
3. 2 cloves garlic;
4. Juice of 1 lemon;
5. 1/4 cup sesame tahini,
6. 1 teaspoon ground cumin;
7. 1 teaspoon paprika;
8. and Salt and ground black pepper to taste.

Instructions:
1. Place all ingredients in a food processor and blend until smooth.
2. Taste and adjust the seasoning if desired.
3. Serve the hummus with pita bread, chips or vegetables.

Nutrition Information:

Serving size - 1/2 cup. Calories - 114, Protein - 4g, Fat - 5g, Carbs - 11g, Sodium - 175mg.

31. Creamy Pea and Potato Soup

Creamy Pea and Potato Soup is a delicious and nutritious meal that's perfect for a chilly evening. This tasty soup comes together quickly and requires only a few simple ingredients.
Serving: 4
| Preparation Time: 10 minutes
| Ready Time: 30 minutes

Ingredients:
- 2 tablespoons olive oil
- 1 yellow onion, diced
- 2 cups potatoes, peeled and diced
- 1 cup frozen peas
- 4 cups vegetable broth
- 2 tablespoons fresh dill, chopped
- Salt and pepper to taste

Instructions:
1. Heat olive oil in a large pot over medium heat.
2. Add diced onion to pot and cook for about 4 minutes, until softened.
3. Add potatoes and frozen peas to pot and stir to combine.
4. Pour vegetable broth into pot and bring to a boil.
5. Reduce heat and simmer for 20 minutes, or until potatoes are softened.
6. Use an immersion blender to puree soup until smooth. Stir in chopped dill and season with salt and pepper to taste.
7. Serve hot.

Nutrition Information (per serving):
Calories: 110, Total Fat: 5g, Saturated Fat: 1g, Sodium: 220mg, Carbohydrates: 13g, Fiber: 3g, Protein: 3g.

32. Penne with Roasted Red Pepper Sauce

This decadent and flavorful Penne with Roasted Red Pepper Sauce is sure to dazzle any dinner table. Featuring fresh and savory ingredients, it can be prepared in under 30 minutes and serves 4-6.

Serving: 4-6
| Preparation Time: 10 minutes
| Ready Time: 20 minutes

Ingredients:
- 2 red bell peppers
- 2 cloves garlic, minced
- 3 tablespoons olive oil
- 1 teaspoon salt
- 2 shallots, chopped
- 2 tablespoons parsley, chopped
- 2 tablespoons Parmesan cheese, freshly grated
- 2 tablespoons basil, chopped
- 3 tablespoons balsamic vinegar
- 1/2 teaspoon black pepper
- 2 cups heavy cream
- 12 ounces penne pasta

Instructions:
1. Preheat the oven to 375F. Cut the bell peppers in half, removing any seeds. Arrange cut side up in a baking dish and roast for 25 minutes.
2. While the peppers are roasting, heat the olive oil in a medium-size pot over medium-heat and add the garlic, salt, and shallots. Saute for 3-4 minutes until shallots are translucent.
3. Add the parsley, Parmesan cheese, basil, balsamic vinegar, and black pepper. Stir to combine.
4. Add the heavy cream and reduce heat to low. Simmer for 5 minutes, stirring occasionally.
5. When peppers are finished roasting, remove from oven and peel away the skins. Chop into 1-inch pieces and add to the pot. Simmer for 5 minutes.
6. Boil the penne according to package instructions until al dente.
7. Drain the pasta and add to the pot with the sauce. Stir to combine. Serve hot.

Nutrition Information:
Per serving: 563 calories; 36.7 g fat; 20.6 g carbohydrates; 28.9 g protein.

33. Noodle Bowl with Pork and Vegetables

A classic and delicious noodle bowl with pork, vegetables and a flavorful sauce is sure to hit the spot. This easy-peasy dish is a great meal option for lunch or dinner.
Serving: Serves 3-4
| Preparation Time: 10 minutes
| Ready Time: 20 minutes

Ingredients:
- 8oz pork strips
- 4 cloves garlic, minced
- 2 tablespoons soy sauce
- 2 tablespoons oyster sauce
- 2 tablespoons hoisin sauce
- 2 tablespoons vegetable oil
- 6 cups vegetable stock
- 8oz egg noodles
- 2 carrots, finely diced
- 2 zucchini, finely diced
- 2 cups bean sprouts
- 1 onion, finely diced
- 1 green bell pepper, finely diced
- Salt and pepper, to taste
- 2 tablespoons sesame oil
- 1 tablespoon sesame seeds

Instructions:
1. Heat a large skillet over medium heat and add pork strips. Cook until lightly browned, about 5 minutes. Add garlic and cook for another minute.
2. Add soy sauce, oyster sauce, hoisin sauce and vegetable oil and cook until combined, about 3 minutes.
3. In a large saucepan, bring vegetable stock to a boil and add egg noodles. Cook according to package directions, about 8 minutes. Drain.

4. Once pork is cooked, add carrots, zucchini, bean sprouts, onion, and bell pepper to the skillet. Cook until vegetables are tender, about 5 minutes.

5. Add noodles to the vegetables and pork and cook until heated through, about 2 minutes.

6. Remove from heat and season with salt and pepper, to taste.

7. Add sesame oil and sesame seeds and toss to combine.

8. Serve immediately.

Nutrition Information:
Per serving (237g) - 226 Calories, 11g Fat, 17g Carbs, 16g Protein.

34. Chicken Tikka Masala

Chicken Tikka Masala is a delicious and popular Indian dish that consists of marinated chicken cooked in a creamy, spicy tomato sauce. It is hearty, savory, and fragrant, and is sure to become a favorite in your household.

Servings: 4
| Preparation Time: 20 minutes
| Ready in: 40 minutes

Ingredients:
- 2 lbs boneless, skinless chicken thighs, cut into 1-inch cubes
- 1 head garlic, minced
- 2 tablespoons garam masala
- 2 tablespoons ginger, minced
- 2 tablespoons vegetable oil
- 1 onion, diced
- 2 tablespoons tomato paste
- 1 can of diced tomatoes
- 1 cup heavy cream
- Salt and pepper to taste

Instructions:
1. In a bowl, mix together the chicken cubes with garlic, garam masala and ginger. Allow to sit for at least 15 minutes.

2. Heat the oil in a large skillet over medium heat. Add in the marinated chicken and onion and cook until the chicken is lightly browned and the onion is soft and translucent.
3. Stir in tomato paste and tomatoes, and simmer for 10 minutes.
4. Reduce the heat and stir in heavy cream, simmering for an additional 10 minutes.
5. Season with salt and pepper to taste.

Nutrition Information:
Per Serving: 290 calories; 13.4 g fat; 19 g carbohydrates; 22.4 g protein.

35. Thai Red Curry

A popular Thai dish, Thai Red Curry is made with a mix of red curry paste and coconut milk that create an incredible comforting and richly spiced dish.
Serving: 4
| Preparation Time: 15 minutes
| Ready Time: 55 minutes

Ingredients:
- 2 tablespoons red curry paste
- 2 tablespoons vegetable oil
- 1 can coconut milk
- 1 medium onion, thinly sliced
- 1 teaspoon minced garlic
- 2 tablespoons fish sauce
- 2 carrots, chopped
- 2 cups diced potatoes
- 1 bell pepper, sliced
- 1 red or green chili, sliced (optional)
- 1/2 bunch fresh Thai basil leaves

Instructions:
1. Heat the oil in a large pot over medium heat.
2. Add the red curry paste and stir fry until fragrant, about 1 minute.
3. Add the onion and garlic and fry for another minute.
4. Add the coconut milk and bring to a boil.

5. Add the fish sauce and vegetables.
6. Lower the heat and simmer for 30 minutes, stirring occasionally.
7. Add the Thai basil leaves and simmer for an additional 5 minutes.

Nutrition Information:
Per Serving: Calories: 287; Fat: 19.6g; Carbohydrates: 21.4g; Protein: 7.7g; Cholesterol: 0mg; Sodium: 596mg.

36. Shepherd's Pie

Shepherd's Pie is an easy and delicious meal that takes just 30 minutes of | Preparation Time and 35 minutes total to prepare. This classic English dish is perfect for nights when hearty comfort food is needed. It serves 8 people and is a rich and filling dish that combines ground beef and vegetables in a creamy gravy topped with fluffy mashed potatoes.
Serving: 8
| Preparation Time: 30 minutes
| Ready Time: 35 minutes

Ingredients:
1. 2 tablespoons olive oil
2. 1 large onion, diced
3. 1/2 cup carrots, diced
4. 1/2 cup celery, diced
5. 2 cloves garlic, minced
6. 1 pound ground beef
7. 4 tablespoons all-purpose flour
8. 1 teaspoon fresh thyme
9. 2 tablespoons tomato paste
10. 2 cups beef broth
11. 1 cup frozen green peas
12. 2 tablespoons Worcestershire sauce
13. 2 tablespoons butter
14. 2 tablespoons sour cream
15. 1 teaspoon salt
16. 1 teaspoon pepper
17. 3 large potatoes
18. 1/2 cup milk

Instructions:
1. Preheat oven to 425F.
2. Heat olive oil in a large Dutch oven over medium heat. Add onion, carrots, celery, and garlic and cook until vegetables are softened, about 5 minutes.
3. Add ground beef, breaking it up with a spoon as it cooks, until beef is browned and cooked through.
4. Add flour, thyme, and tomato paste and cook for 1 minute.
5. Add beef broth, peas, Worcestershire sauce, and butter. Bring to a boil and reduce heat to simmer. Cook uncovered for about 10 minutes until sauce has thickened.
6. Meanwhile, peel and chop potatoes into 1-inch cubes and place in a large pot. Fill pot with cold water so potatoes are just covered. Bring to a boil and cook for 10 minutes or until potatoes are soft.
7. Drain potatoes and place back in pot. Add sour cream, salt and pepper, and milk. Mash until smooth and creamy.
8. Spread beef mixture in an 11x13-inch baking pan. Spread mashed potatoes over beef.
9. Bake in preheated oven for 25 minutes or until golden brown.

Nutrition Information (per serving):
Calories: 450, Total Fat: 21.5 g, Cholesterol: 70 mg, Sodium: 710 mg, Carbohydrate: 33 g, Fiber: 5 g, Protein: 27 g

37. Baked Mac and Cheese

Baked Mac and Cheese is a creamy, indulgent dish best served hot straight out of the oven. For those looking for a comforting, cheesy classic with a crunchy topping, this is the dish for you!
Serves 6. | Preparation Time: 15 minutes, | Ready Time: 30 minutes.

Ingredients:
- 8 ounces macaroni
- 2 tablespoons butter
- 1/4 cup all-purpose flour
- 2 cups milk
- 1 teaspoon Dijon mustard

- Salt and ground black pepper to taste
- 1/4 teaspoon garlic powder
- 1/4 teaspoon onion powder
- 1 (8 ounce) package shredded extra sharp Cheddar cheese, divided
- 2 tablespoons grated Parmesan cheese

Instructions:
1. Preheat oven to 350 degrees F (175 degrees C). Grease a 2-quart baking dish.
2. Cook macaroni in a pot of lightly salted boiling water according to package directions; drain and set aside.
3. Melt butter in a saucepan over medium heat; stir in flour until smooth, then gradually mix in milk, 1/2 cup at a time. Bring to a boil, reduce heat to low, and cook until mixture is thick, stirring constantly.
4. Remove saucepan from heat, and stir in mustard, salt, pepper, garlic powder, onion powder and 2/3 of the Cheddar cheese until melted.
5. In the prepared baking dish, stir together cooked macaroni and cheese sauce; top with remaining Cheddar cheese and Parmesan cheese.
6. Bake in preheated oven for 20 minutes, or until cheese is melted and golden brown.

Nutrition Information:
Per Serving – 495 calories, 20 g fat, 62 mg cholesterol, 505 mg sodium, 53 g carbohydrates, 4 g dietary fiber and 24 g protein.

38. Chicken and Asparagus Risotto

Chicken and Asparagus Risotto is a delicious Italian-style main dish with a creamy texture. This simple risotto is loaded with tender chicken, fresh asparagus, and flavorful parmesan cheese.
Serving: 6
| Preparation Time: 20 minutes
| Ready Time: 35 minutes

Ingredients:
- 1 tablespoon olive oil
- 1 large onion, diced
- 2 garlic cloves, minced

- 2 cups arborio rice
- 1/2 cup white wine
- 6 cups chicken broth
- 1/2 cup Parmesan cheese, grated
- 2 cups cooked chicken, diced
- 1/2 pound steamed asparagus, chopped
- Salt and pepper to taste

Instructions:
1. Heat the oil in a large pot over medium heat.
Add the onions and cook, stirring occasionally, until softened, about 5 minutes.
2. Add the garlic and cook one more minute.
3. Add the arborio rice and cook, stirring, for 2 minutes.
4. Pour in the white wine and cook, stirring, until the wine has been absorbed.
5. Add the chicken broth, 1 cup at a time, stirring constantly. Cook until the broth has been absorbed each time before adding more.
6. Once all the broth has been added, reduce the heat to low and stir in the Parmesan cheese and cooked chicken.
7. Add the asparagus and season with salt and pepper. Cook for a few more minutes, until the risotto is creamy and all the ingredients are heated through.
8. Serve hot.

Nutrition Information: (per serving)
265 calories, 7.6g fat, 32.2g carbs, 2.9g fiber, 13.1g protein

39. Potato Pancakes

Potato pancakes make for a comforting, delicious side dish. These savory spuds are easy to whip up and pair perfectly with just about any meal.
Serving: Makes 12 pancakes
| Preparation Time: 5 minutes
| Ready Time: 30 minutes

Ingredients:
-3 large potatoes, grated or shredded

-2 tablespoons of onion, diced
-1 egg, beaten
-Salt and pepper, to taste
-2 tablespoons of all-purpose flour
-Vegetable oil, for frying

Instructions:
1. In a large bowl, mix the grated potatoes with onion, egg, salt, and pepper.
2. Cover the bowl with a cloth and leave aside for 15 minutes.
3. After 15 minutes, add flour to the bowl and mix everything.
4. Take a spoonful of the mixture and form it into an oval-shaped pancake.
5. Heat oil in a skillet and fry the potato pancakes on both sides until they are golden and crispy.
6. Serve hot and enjoy!

Nutrition Information:
Each Potato Pancake has 110 calories, 2.5g fat, 18g carbohydrates, and 2g protein.

40. Red Pepper and Spinach Pizza

This tasty Red Pepper and Spinach Pizza is a fantastic way to treat your taste buds with some serious flavor. Packed with sweetness from the Red Pepper and nutritional benefits of Spinach, this easy to make pizza is sure to please the whole family!
Serving: 4
| Preparation Time: 10 minutes
| Ready Time: 15 - 20 minutes

Ingredients:
- 250g of Pizza Dough
- 1 Chopped Red Pepper
- 2 Handfuls of Spinach
- 1/2 cup of Tomato Sauce
- 2 tablespoons of Olive Oil
- Salt & Pepper to Taste

Instructions:

1. Preheat the oven to 200°C and line a baking tray with greaseproof paper.
2. Roll out the pizza dough and place onto the greaseproof paper.
3. Spread the tomato sauce evenly over the pizza base.
4. Sprinkle the chopped red pepper and spinach over the top.
5. Drizzle the olive oil over the top and season to taste.
6. Bake in the oven for 15-20 minutes until the base is golden and crispy.

Nutrition Information Per Serving:

Calories – 316kcal
Protein – 9.3g
Fat – 7.3g
Carbohydrates – 50.3g

41. Ratatouille

Ratatouille is a hearty and flavorful French stew made with fresh vegetables like zucchini, eggplant, bell peppers, tomatoes, and onions, simmered in a tomato-based broth.

Serving: 4-6
| Preparation Time: 10 minutes
| Ready Time: 35 minutes

Ingredients:

- 2 tablespoons olive oil
- 1 onion, diced
- 2 cloves garlic, minced
- 1 zucchini, diced
- 1 eggplant, diced
- 1 red bell pepper, diced
- 1 yellow bell pepper, diced
- 2 cups canned diced tomatoes
- 2 tablespoons fresh parsley, chopped
- 2 teaspoons dried oregano
- 1 teaspoon salt
- 1/2 teaspoon freshly ground black pepper

Instructions:
1. Heat the oil in a large saucepan over medium heat. Add the onion, garlic, zucchini, eggplant, and bell peppers, and cook until the vegetables are softened, about 5 minutes.
2. Add the tomatoes, parsley, oregano, salt, and pepper, and bring to a simmer. Simmer until the vegetables are tender, about 25 minutes.
3. Serve over cooked noodles, rice, or quinoa. Enjoy!

Nutrition Information:
Calories: 123; fat: 5g; carbohydrates: 19g; protein: 3g; fiber: 5g

42. Seared Tuna with Avocado Salsa

Seared Tuna with Avocado Salsa is a delicious and healthy dish perfect for hot summer nights. It combines a classic combination of flavors, creating a balance between rich peppery tuna and creamy avocado salsa. This dish is sure to be a hit on your table!
Serving: 4
| Preparation Time: 15 minutes
| Ready Time: 45 minutes

Ingredients:
1.   4 six-ounce tuna steaks
2.   Salt and pepper, to taste
3.   1 tablespoon olive oil
4.   1 avocado, diced
5.   1/2 red onion, minced
6.   2 tablespoons fresh lime juice
7.   1 jalapeno pepper, seeded and minced
8.   2 tablespoons chopped fresh cilantro

Instructions:
1. Rinse the tuna steaks and pat dry. Season with salt and pepper, to taste.
2. Heat a large skillet over high heat and add the olive oil. Sear the tuna steaks for approximately 2 minutes per side, or until golden brown and cooked through.

3. In a medium bowl, combine the avocado, red onion, lime juice, jalapeno pepper, and cilantro. Mix until evenly combined.
4. Serve the tuna steaks with a generous topping of avocado salsa.

Nutrition Information:
Calories: 200, Fat: 9g, Cholesterol: 30mg, Sodium: 270mg, Carbohydrates: 6g, Protein: 22g, Potassium: 510mg.

43. Quinoa-Stuffed Bell Peppers

Quinoa-Stuffed Bell Peppers are an incredibly tasty and incredibly healthy meal that is quick to make and full of flavor. The perfect dish for lunch or dinner, the bell peppers are stuffed with nutritious quinoa and topped with your favorite cheeses. Enjoy this meal with a side of vegetables and a light salad.
Serving: 4
| Preparation Time: 10 minutes
| Ready Time: 35 minutes

Ingredients:
- 4 large bell peppers
- 1 teaspoon olive oil
- 1/2 cup chopped onion
- 1 1/2 cups cooked quinoa
- 1 teaspoon chili powder
- 1/2 teaspoon smoked paprika
- 2 cloves garlic, minced
- 1/2 teaspoon dried oregano
- 1 cup vegetable broth
- 1 15-ounce can black beans, drained and rinsed
- 1 cup cooked corn kernels
- Salt and pepper, to taste
- 1/4 cup shaved Parmesan cheese, for topping

Instructions:
1. Preheat oven to 375F. Halve bell peppers and remove ribs and seeds.
2. In a large skillet, heat olive oil over medium heat and cook onion for 3-4 minutes, until softened.

3. Add cooked quinoa, chili powder, smoked paprika, garlic, oregano, vegetable broth, black beans, corn kernels, salt and pepper to the pan with the onions. Cook, stirring occasionally, for 7-8 minutes, until all ingredients are combined.
4. Fill bell peppers with quinoa mixture. Top with shaved Parmesan.
5. Bake for 25-30 minutes, or until bell peppers are tender. Serve immediately.

Nutrition Information (per serving):
Calories: 239; Total Fat: 5.8g; Saturated Fat: 1.9g; Cholesterol: 13mg; Sodium: 326mg; Carbohydrate: 35.2g; Dietary Fiber: 8.6g; Protein: 11.7g

44. Pumpkin Soup

This creamy and comforting Pumpkin Soup is made with simple ingredients and easy to make. Serve with a side of crusty bread for a perfect Autumn dinner.
Serving: 6-8
| Preparation Time: 15 minutes
| Ready Time: 30 minutes

Ingredients:
- 2 tablespoons olive oil
- 1 onion, diced
- 2 carrots, peeled and diced
- 2 celery stalks, diced
- 4 cups pumpkin puree
- 4 cups vegetable stock
- 1 teaspoon dried thyme
- 1 teaspoon salt
- 1/2 teaspoon black pepper

Instructions:
1. Heat oil in a large pot over medium heat. Add the onion, carrot, and celery and cook for 5 minutes, until softened.

2. Add the pumpkin puree, vegetable stock, thyme, salt and black pepper and stir to combine. Bring to a boil, then reduce the heat and simmer for 20 minutes.
3. Carefully ladle the soup into a blender (or use an immersion blender) and blend until smooth. Serve hot.

Nutrition Information:
Per serving (1.5 cups): Calories 161, Total Fat 6 g (Saturated 1 g, Polyunsaturated 2 g, Monounsaturated 3 g), Cholesterol 0 mg, Sodium 531 mg, Potassium 551 mg, Total Carbohydrate 26 g, Dietary Fiber 4 g, Protein 4 g.

45. Fajitas

Fajitas are a Southwestern dish traditionally made of grilled marinated chicken, beef, shrimp, or vegetables served in a warm tortilla. This delicious dish is packed with flavor and can be incredibly versatile. Serve it as a light meal or make a spread for party guests!
Serving: 6
| Preparation Time: 15 minutes
| Ready Time: 25 minutes

Ingredients:
• 1 pound chicken or beef
• 1 large onion
• 2 bell peppers (red, green, or yellow)
• 2 tablespoons of olive oil
• 2 tablespoons of chili powder
• 1 tablespoon of ground cumin
• 1 teaspoon of garlic powder
• 6 large flour or corn tortillas
• Salt and freshly ground pepper to taste

Instructions:
1. Cut the chicken or beef into thin strips.
2. In a bowl, combine the chili powder, ground cumin, garlic powder, oil, salt and pepper. Add the chicken or beef strips to the mixture and stir to coat evenly.

3. Heat a large skillet over medium heat. When hot, add the chicken or beef, onion, and peppers. Cook for 4-5 minutes, stirring occasionally.
4. Meanwhile, warm the tortillas either in a microwave or in a warm skillet.
5. Spoon the chicken or beef, onion, and peppers onto the warm tortillas.
6. Garnish with extra chili powder, guacamole, shredded cheese, sour cream, salsa, or any other favorite toppings.

Nutrition Information (per serving):
Calories: 270, Total fat: 9g, Cholesterol: 70mg, Sodium: 270mg, Protein: 26g, Carbohydrates: 18g, Fiber: 4g, Sugar: 2g.

46. Tomato and Herbed Ricotta Tart

Tomato and Herbed Ricotta Tart is a flavorful and delicious dish. Boasting a medley of fresh flavors, this tart has a golden crunchy crust filled with a creamy herbed ricotta and tomato center. A beautiful appetizer or main course, this simple but extraordinary tart will leave your party guests wanting more.
Serving: 8
| Preparation Time: 15 minutes
| Ready Time: 35 minutes

Ingredients:
- 1 package of pre-made pie crust
- 1 cup whole-milk ricotta cheese
- 2 tablespoons finely chopped fresh herbs (such as basil, oregano, and rosemary)
- 1/4 teaspoon salt
- Freshly ground black pepper, to taste
- 2 to 3 large tomatoes, sliced thin
- 2 tablespoons extra-virgin olive oil

Instructions:
1. Preheat the oven to 400 degrees Fahrenheit.
2. Place the pie crust into a 9-inch tart pan and press lightly into the sides to form a crust.

3. In a medium bowl, combine ricotta, herbs, salt and pepper. Spread the mixture over the bottom of the crust.
4. Lay the tomato slices over the ricotta and season with additional salt, pepper and herbs, as desired.
5. Drizzle the olive oil over the tomatoes and bake for 30 minutes, or until the crust is a golden brown and tomatoes are cooked through.
6. Let cool before slicing and serving.

Nutrition Information (per serving):
Calories: 186; Total Fat: 11 g; Saturated Fat: 4 g; Cholesterol: 14 mg; Sodium: 294 mg; Carbohydrates: 16 g; Protein: 6 g; Dietary Fiber: 1 g; Sugar: 2 g.

47. Seven Layer Salad

Seven Layer Salad is a classic layered salad with a mix of flavors and textures. It is a perfect choice for potlucks and backyard barbecues. It is easy to prepare and can be enjoyed chilled or at room temperature.
Serving: 12, | Preparation Time: 10 minutes, | Ready Time: 2 hours

Ingredients:
-6 cups of lettuce
-3 hard boiled eggs, chopped
-1 cup grated cheddar cheese
-1/2 cup sliced tomatoes
-1/2 cup finely chopped celery
-1/2 cup peas
-1/2 cup chopped green onions
-1/2 cup mayonnaise
-1/2 cup sour cream

Instructions:
1. In a large bowl, combine the lettuce, eggs, cheese, tomatoes, celery, peas, and green onions. Mix together until all ingredients are evenly distributed.
2. In a separate bowl, combine the mayonnaise and sour cream. Spread the mixture over the salad and mix until evenly coated.

3. Layer the salad in a large, deep bowl or dish. Cover and refrigerate for at least two hours before serving.

Nutrition Information (per serving):
Calories: 159, Fat: 12.3g, Carbs: 6.2g, Protein: 6.8g, Cholesterol: 81mg, Sodium: 209.7mg

48. Spinach and Artichoke Dip

This creamy Spinach and Artichoke Dip is loaded with rich, cheesy flavors and is the perfect appetizer or side dish.
Serving: 4
| Preparation Time: 5 minutes
| Ready Time: 25 minutes

Ingredients:
- 2 (14 ounce) cans artichoke hearts, drained
-2 cloves garlic, minced
-1 (10 ounce) package frozen chopped spinach, thawed and squeezed dry
-1 (8 ounce) package cream cheese, softened
-1 cup grated Parmesan cheese
-1/2 cup mayonnaise
-2 tablespoons fresh lemon juice
-1/4 teaspoon red pepper flakes

Instructions:
1. Preheat oven to 350 degrees F (175 degrees C).
2. In a medium bowl, mix together artichokes, garlic, spinach, cream cheese, Parmesan cheese, mayonnaise, lemon juice, and red pepper flakes.
3. Transfer mixture to a baking dish, and bake in preheated oven for 25 minutes, or until lightly brown.

Nutrition Information:
Calories: 299 kcal, Carbohydrates: 7 g, Protein: 8 g, Fat: 26 g, Saturated Fat: 9 g, Cholesterol: 37 mg, Sodium: 592 mg, Potassium: 131 mg, Fiber: 3 g, Sugar: 1 g, Vitamin A: 2595 IU, Vitamin C: 5.4 mg, Calcium: 224 mg, Iron: 1.4 mg.

49. Arancini Balls

Arancini Balls are a classic Italian street food dish made from risotto and filled with delicious cheese and sometimes other ingredients. The bite-size snacks are golden-brown and incredibly flavorful. They are perfect for a snack or appetizer at a party!

Serving: 8-12 Arancini Balls
| Preparation Time: 20 minutes
| Ready Time: 25 minutes

Ingredients:
-1 cup of cooked risotto
-1/2 cup of shredded mozzarella cheese
-1/4 cup of grated Parmesan cheese
-2 tablespoons of parsley, finely chopped
-Salt and pepper to taste
-1 egg, beaten lightly
-1/2 cup of all-purpose flour
-1 cup of plain breadcrumbs
-3-4 tablespoons of olive oil for frying

Instructions:
1. In a bowl mix together cooked risotto, mozzarella, parmesan, parsley, salt and pepper until ingredients are well combined.
2. Shape the mixture into balls of desired size and set on a plate.
3. Prepare a shallow bowl with the beaten egg, another with the flour, and the third with the breadcrumbs.
4. Heat the oil in a frying pan over medium heat.
5. Dip the risotto balls in the egg, then in the flour, and then in the breadcrumbs.
6. Fry the balls in batches until golden-brown and crispy.
7. Drain on paper towels and serve warm.

Nutrition Information:
Calories: 204
Fat: 7.7 g
Carbohydrates: 24.2 g

Protein: 8.3 g

50. Chili-Rubbed Pork Tenderloin

Chili-Rubbed Pork Tenderloin is a delicious and easy meal perfect for a weeknight dinner. It packs a punch with a zesty combination of chili powder, garlic and oregano. The spices complement the mild pork tenderloin for a flavorful and moist dish.
Serving: 6
| Preparation Time: 10 minutes
| Ready Time: 45 minutes

Ingredients:
-1 1/2-2 pounds pork tenderloin
-1 tablespoon chili powder
-1 teaspoon garlic powder
-1/2 teaspoon oregano
-1/4 teaspoon salt
-1 tablespoon olive oil

Instructions:
1. Preheat oven to 375F.
2. Pat pork tenderloin dry with a paper towel. In a small bowl, combine chili powder, garlic powder, oregano and salt. Rub the seasoning all over the pork.
3. Heat oil in a large cast iron skillet over medium-high heat. When the oil is hot, add the pork tenderloin and brown it on all sides, about 2 minutes per side.
4. Place the skillet in the oven and cook for 20-25 minutes, until the internal temperature of the pork reaches 145F.
5. Let the pork rest for 5 minutes before slicing and serving.

Nutrition Information:
Serving Size: 1/6 of Pork Tenderloin
Calories: 205
Protein: 28g
Carbohydrates: 1g
Fat: 8g

51. Pulled Pork Sandwiches

Pulled Pork Sandwiches are a meal that is both flavorful and fragrant, perfect for any time of year. These sandwiches can be served as a main dish or as an appetizer to larger meals, and will please even the pickiest of eaters. The prep time for this meal is relatively short, allowing for plenty of time for the pulled pork to cook and become soft and juicy.
Serves: 4; | Preparation Time: 10 minutes; | Ready Time: 45 minutes;

Ingredients:
-2.5 lb pork tenderloin
-1/2 onion, chopped
-1/2 cup barbecue sauce
-1/2 cup tomato sauce
-8 hamburger buns

Instructions:
1. Preheat oven to 375F.
2. Place tenderloin into a large baking dish.
3. Add onion, barbecue sauce, and tomato sauce to the baking dish.
4. Bake uncovered for 40 minutes or until pork is cooked through.
5. Remove from oven and let cool. Once cooled, shred pork with a fork.
6. Serve pulled pork on hamburger buns with additional barbecue and/or tomato sauce, if desired.

Nutrition Information:
Serving Size: 1 sandwich
Calories: 300
Total Fat: 8 g
Saturated Fat: 3 g
Cholesterol: 75 mg
Sodium: 700 mg
Carbohydrates: 30 g
Fiber: 4 g
Protein: 20 g

52. Crustless Quiche

Crustless Quiche is a delicious and versatile meal that is easy to make for breakfast, brunch and even dinner. This quiche is made without any crust, making it a great option for those looking for a lighter meal.
Serving 6, | Preparation Time 10 minutes, Ready in 40 minutes.

Ingredients
- 4 eggs
- 2 cups dairy (skim milk, almond milk, cream)
- 1/2 teaspoon dry mustard
- 1/2 teaspoon salt
- 1 cup shredded cheese
- 1/4 cup diced vegetables (spinach, peppers, mushrooms, onions, etc.)

Instructions:
1. Preheat oven to 350 degrees
2. In a bowl, whisk together eggs and dairy, mustard, salt and pepper.
3. Pour egg mixture into greased 9 inch pie dish.
4. Sprinkle the cheese and diced vegetables evenly over the top.
5. Bake in preheated oven until the top is golden brown and the center is set, about 30 to 40 minutes.
6. Allow to cool 10 minutes before cutting and serving.

Nutrition Information:
Each serving contains 127 Calories, 8g Fat, 5g Protein, 8g Carbohydrates, 0g Fiber and 703mg Sodium.

53. Creamy Polenta

Creamy Polenta is a classic Italian side dish made from cooked cornmeal and quick to prepare. Serve it with braised meats, mushrooms, and plenty of Parmesan cheese for a comforting meal.
Serving: 6
| Preparation Time: 10 minutes
| Ready Time: 20 minutes

Ingredients:

- 3 cups water
- 1 cup yellow cornmeal
- 2 tablespoons butter
- 1 tablespoon olive oil
- 1 teaspoon kosher salt
- 1/3 cup freshly grated Parmesan cheese

Instructions:
1. Bring 3 cups of water to a boil in a large saucepan.
2. Reduce heat to low, and slowly pour in the yellow cornmeal, stirring constantly.
3. Continue stirring the mixture for 15 minutes, until the polenta thickens and pulls away from the sides of the pot.
4. Turn off the heat and stir in the butter, olive oil, salt, and Parmesan cheese, stirring until all the ingredients are fully combined.

Nutrition Information:
Calories: 190, Fat: 7g, Carbohydrates: 26g , Protein: 5g, Sodium: 290mg

54. Butternut Squash and Sage Risotto

Butternut Squash and Sage Risotto - This creamy and delicious vegan risotto is filled with nourishing butternut squash and fragrant sage, and is sure to delight even the pickiest of eaters.
Serving: 4-6 people
| Preparation Time: 45 minutes
| Ready Time: 1 hour

Ingredients:
- 2 tablespoons olive oil
- 1 onion, finely chopped
- 1 garlic clove, crushed
- 1 teaspoon dried sage
- 300g (10oz) risotto rice
- 800ml (1 pint 10fl oz) hot vegetable stock
- 450g (1lb) butternut squash cubes
- 25g (1oz) vegan butter
- 4-6 tablespoons of vegan grated parmesan

Instructions:

1. Heat the oil in a large saucepan, add the onion and cook for 5 minutes, stirring occasionally. Add the garlic and sage and cook for an additional minute.

2. Add the risotto rice to the pan and coat in the oil. Gradually add ladles of the hot vegetable stock, stirring until it has all been absorbed.

3. Add the butternut squash cubes and cook for 15-20 minutes, stirring occasionally, until the rice is cooked and creamy.

4. Add the vegan butter and vegan grated parmesan and stir through.

5. Serve in warm bowls and enjoy.

Nutrition Information:

per serving – Energy: 260 kcal, Fat: 12.1g, Carbohydrates: 28.3g, Protein: 7.3g, Fibre: 2.7g, Salt: 0.9g.

55. Grilled Vegetable Kebabs

Grilled Vegetable Kebabs are a delicious and healthy summer meal that is easy to make and sure to please. This recipe serves 4 and is ready to eat in 35 minutes, plus 10 minutes of preparation.

Serving: 4

| Preparation Time: 10 minutes

| Ready Time: 35 minutes

Ingredients:

- 2 red bell peppers, cut into 1-inch pieces
- 2 zucchinis, cut into 1-inch pieces
- 2 red onions, cut into 1-inch pieces
- 2 tablespoons olive oil
- 1 teaspoon garlic powder
- 1 teaspoon Italian seasoning
- 1/4 teaspoon salt
- 1/4 teaspoon pepper

Instructions:

1. Preheat the grill or grill pan to medium-high heat.

2. In a large bowl, combine the bell peppers, zucchini, and onion.

3. Drizzle the vegetables with olive oil, garlic powder, Italian seasoning, salt, and pepper.
4. Stir the vegetables to coat with the oil and spices.
5. Place the vegetables on the preheated grill.
6. Grill for 10 minutes, flipping once halfway through.
7. Remove from the grill and serve.

Nutrition Information (per serving):
Calories: 150
Fat: 7 g
Carbohydrates: 16 g
Protein: 3 g
Sodium: 205 mg

56. Banana Bread

Banana bread is a classic, easy-to-make treat that makes a delicious breakfast, snack, or even dessert. This delicious recipe requires very simple ingredients and low effort.
Serving: 8-10 slices
| Preparation Time: 10 minutes
| Ready Time: 45 minutes

Ingredients:
-3 very ripe bananas, mashed
-1/3 cup melted butter
-3/4 cup sugar
-1 egg, beaten
-1 teaspoon vanilla extract
-1 teaspoon baking soda
-2 cups all-purpose flour

Instructions:
1. Preheat the oven to 350 degrees F (175 degrees C). Grease a 9x5 inch loaf pan.
2. In a medium bowl, stir together the mashed banana, melted butter, sugar, egg and vanilla extract.

3. In a separate bowl, whisk together the baking soda and the flour. Add the flour mixture to the banana mixture, and stir until combined.
4.Pour the batter into the prepared loaf pan.
5. Bake in the preheated oven for 40-45 minutes, or until a knife inserted into the center of the loaf comes out clean.

Nutrition Information:
Per serving: 209 calories; 8.7 g fat; 28.9 g carbohydrates; 3.2 g protein; 36 mg cholesterol; 143 mg sodium.

57. Chicken Enchiladas

Chicken Enchiladas: An easy and flavorful Mexican-inspired dish.
Serving: 4
| Preparation Time: 10 minutes
| Ready Time: 30 minutes

Ingredients:
1.   2 cups cooked, shredded chicken
2.   1 16-ounce can enchilada sauce
3.   1/2 cup chopped onion
4.   1 5-ounce can sliced olives
5.   1 4-ounce can diced green chilies
6.   8-12 6-inch corn tortillas
7.   1/2 cup shredded cheese

Instructions:
1. Preheat oven to 350 degrees.
2. In a large bowl, mix together chicken, onion, olives, and green chilies.
3. Into each tortilla shell, place 1/4 cup of chicken mixture. Roll the shells tightly, and place seam side down into a baking dish.
4. Pour the enchilada sauce over the shells, and top with cheese.
5. Bake in preheated oven for 25 – 30 minutes.

Nutrition Information:
Calories: 360, Total Fat: 8 g, Cholesterol: 70 mg, Sodium: 480 mg, Total Carbohydrates: 41 g, Protein: 24 g.

58. Thai Peanut Noodles

For a Thai-inspired dish, try this delicious and easy-to-make Thai Peanut Noodles. This dish is packed with flavour and makes a great meal for a group or potluck.
Serving: Serves 4
| Preparation Time: 10 minutes
| Ready Time: 15 minutes

Ingredients:
- 8 ounces dry spaghetti noodles
- 1/4 cup smooth peanut butter
- 2 tablespoons soy sauce
- 2 tablespoons rice vinegar
- 2 tablespoons sesame oil
- 1 tablespoon honey
- 2 cloves garlic, minced
- 1 teaspoon grated fresh ginger
- 1/2 teaspoon crushed red pepper flakes
- 1/4 cup chopped fresh cilantro
- 1/4 cup chopped green onions

Instructions:
1. Cook the spaghetti according to package instructions.
2. In a medium bowl, whisk together the peanut butter, soy sauce, rice vinegar, sesame oil, honey, garlic, and ginger.
3. When the noodles are done cooking, drain them and rinse with cold water.
4. Toss the noodles in the peanut butter mixture and top with cilantro, green onions, and red pepper flakes.
5. Serve immediately or store in the refrigerator for up to 3 days.

Nutrition Information:
Calories: 464; Fat: 17g; Saturated Fat: 3g; Carbs: 57g; Sugar: 9g; Fiber: 4g; Protein: 17g; Cholesterol: 0mg; Sodium: 714mg.

59. Shepherd's Pie

Shepherd's Pie is an easy and delicious meal that takes just 30 minutes of
| Preparation Time and 35 minutes total to prepare. This classic English
dish is perfect for nights when hearty comfort food is needed. It serves 8
people and is a rich and filling dish that combines ground beef and
vegetables in a creamy gravy topped with fluffy mashed potatoes.
Serving: 8
| Preparation Time: 30 minutes
| Ready Time: 35 minutes

Ingredients:
1. 2 tablespoons olive oil
2. 1 large onion, diced
3. 1/2 cup carrots, diced
4. 1/2 cup celery, diced
5. 2 cloves garlic, minced
6. 1 pound ground beef
7. 4 tablespoons all-purpose flour
8. 1 teaspoon fresh thyme
9. 2 tablespoons tomato paste
10. 2 cups beef broth
11. 1 cup frozen green peas
12. 2 tablespoons Worcestershire sauce
13. 2 tablespoons butter
14. 2 tablespoons sour cream
15. 1 teaspoon salt
16. 1 teaspoon pepper
17. 3 large potatoes
18. 1/2 cup milk

Instructions:
1. Preheat oven to 425F.
2. Heat olive oil in a large Dutch oven over medium heat. Add onion,
carrots, celery, and garlic and cook until vegetables are softened, about 5
minutes.
3. Add ground beef, breaking it up with a spoon as it cooks, until beef is
browned and cooked through.
4. Add flour, thyme, and tomato paste and cook for 1 minute.

5. Add beef broth, peas, Worcestershire sauce, and butter. Bring to a boil and reduce heat to simmer. Cook uncovered for about 10 minutes until sauce has thickened.

6. Meanwhile, peel and chop potatoes into 1-inch cubes and place in a large pot. Fill pot with cold water so potatoes are just covered. Bring to a boil and cook for 10 minutes or until potatoes are soft.

7. Drain potatoes and place back in pot. Add sour cream, salt and pepper, and milk. Mash until smooth and creamy.

8. Spread beef mixture in an 11x13-inch baking pan. Spread mashed potatoes over beef.

9. Bake in preheated oven for 25 minutes or until golden brown.

Nutrition Information (per serving):
Calories: 450, Total Fat: 21.5 g, Cholesterol: 70 mg, Sodium: 710 mg, Carbohydrate: 33 g, Fiber: 5 g, Protein: 27 g

60. Zucchini Fritters

Love the fulfilling taste of savory zucchini? Satisfy cravings with this easy-to-make zucchini fritter recipe. Made with zucchini, garlic, Parmesan cheese, and stuffed with a creamy ricotta filling, these fritters look amazing and taste even better.
Serving: 4
| Preparation Time: 10 minutes
| Ready Time: 18 minutes

Ingredients:
- 2 medium-sized zucchinis, grated
- 1/4 cup all-purpose flour
- 2 cloves of garlic, minced
- 2 tablespoons of grated Parmesan cheese
- Salt and pepper, to taste
- 1/2 cup ricotta cheese
- 2 eggs, whisked
- Vegetable oil, for frying

Instructions:

1. Using cheesecloth, squeeze as much of the moisture out of the grated zucchini as possible.
2. In a large bowl, combine the zucchini, flour, garlic, Parmesan cheese, and season with salt and pepper.
3. In a medium bowl, mix together the ricotta cheese and eggs.
4. Form the zucchini mixture into small patties and carefully stuff each one with about a tablespoon of ricotta cheese mixture.
5. In a large skillet over medium-high heat, heat the vegetable oil. Once the oil is hot, add the fritters and cook until golden brown, flipping once during cooking, about 5 minutes per side.

Nutrition Information (per serving):
Calories: 279, Total Fat: 20, Cholesterol: 86, Sodium: 254, Total Carbohydrates: 14, Dietary Fiber: 3, Sugars: 5, Protein: 11

61. Pumpkin Pie

Pumpkin Pie is a classic seasonal favorite, perfect for any Autumnal occasion. This recipe is sure to bring a smile and a delicious taste to your next holiday get-together.
Serving: 8-10.
| Preparation Time: 25 minutes.
| Ready Time: 55 minutes.

Ingredients:
- 2 eggs
- 1 (15 ounce) can pumpkin puree
- 2/3 cup white sugar
- 1/2 teaspoon salt
- 1 teaspoon ground cinnamon
- 1/2 teaspoon ground ginger
- 1/4 teaspoon ground cloves
- 1/2 teaspoon nutmeg
- 1/3 cup evaporated milk
- 1/2 cup butter melted
- 1 (9 inch) unbaked pastry shell

Instructions:

1. Preheat oven to 425 degrees F (220 degrees C).
2. In a medium bowl beat eggs slightly. Stir in pumpkin, sugar, salt, cinnamon, ginger, cloves and nutmeg. Gradually stir in evaporated milk and melted butter.
3. Pour filling into pastry shell.
4. Bake in preheated oven for 15 minutes. Reduce temperature to 350 degrees F (175 degrees C). Bake 25 minutes more.
5. Cool on a wire rack.

Nutrition Information:
Per serving (1/10 of recipe): 270 calories; 11 g fat; 5 g saturated fat; 29 g carbohydrates; 3 g protein; 55 mg cholesterol; 304 mg sodium.

62. Cheesecake

Cheesecake is a classic dessert loved by all! Rich, creamy, and dreamy, it is the perfect ending to any meal.
Serving 8-10, this decadent treat has a | Preparation Time of 30 minutes, and a cooking time of 40 minutes.

Ingredients:
- 2 cups Graham cracker crumbs
- 3 tablespoons granulated sugar
- 1/3 cup melted butter
- 2 (8 ounce) packages cream cheese, softened
- 4 eggs
- 1 cup granulated sugar
- 2 tablespoons all-purpose flour
- 1 teaspoon vanilla extract
- 1 cup sour cream

Instructions:
1. Preheat oven to 350 degrees F (175 degrees C).
2. In a medium bowl, combine graham cracker crumbs, 3 tablespoons of sugar, and melted butter. Mix until it is evenly blended.
Press mixture into a 9 inch springform pan.
3. In a large bowl, mix together cream cheese, remaining 1 cup of sugar, flour, vanilla extract, sour cream, and eggs. Beat until mixture is smooth.

4. Pour mixture into prepared crust.

5. Bake 40 minutes in the preheated oven.

Nutrition Information:

Calories 330; Total Fat 23.3g; Cholesterol 92mg; Sodium 288mg; Total Carbohydrates 24.2g; Protein 4.9g

63. French Toast

French toast is a classic breakfast favorite that is easy to make and sure to please. Made from bread, milk, eggs and a few simple seasonings, this savory dish is perfect for any day of the week.

Serving: 4

| Preparation Time: 10 mins

| Ready Time: 10 mins

Ingredients:

- 4 slices of lightly toasted bread
- 2 eggs
- 1/2 cup milk
- 1 teaspoon cinnamon
- 2 tablespoons butter
- 1/4 teaspoon nutmeg (optional)
- 1/4 teaspoon vanilla extract (optional)

Instructions:

1. Whisk together the eggs, milk, cinnamon, nutmeg (if using) and vanilla extract (if using).

2. In a separate bowl, melt the butter until it's completely liquid.

3. Heat a large skillet over medium-low heat.

4. Dip the toasted bread slices into the egg mixture, coating both sides.

5. Place the coated slices of bread onto the heated skillet.

6. Cook until the bread is golden brown on each side, about 3 to 5 minutes each side.

7. Serve with butter and/or syrup.

Nutrition Information:

Calories: 212; Fat: 9g; Carbohydrates: 24g; Protein: 8g; Sodium: 400mg.

64. Stuffed French Toast

Stuffed French Toast is a delicious breakfast idea perfect for those special occasions. This breakfast dish is made from bread slices filled with a sweet cream cheese mixture, dipped in egg batter and pan-fried until golden. It's even more delicious when topped with a dusting of powdered sugar and a drizzle of syrup.

Serving: 4
| Preparation Time: 20 minutes
| Ready Time: 10 minutes

Ingredients:
- 8 slices of white bread
- 4oz cream cheese, softened
- 2 tablespoons honey
- 2 eggs
- 1/4 cup milk
- 1 teaspoon ground cinnamon
- 1 teaspoon vanilla extract
- Butter, for greasing
- Powdered sugar, to garnish
- Maple syrup, to garnish

Instructions:
1. In a large mixing bowl, using an electric mixer, cream together cream cheese, honey, eggs, milk, ground cinnamon, and vanilla extract.
2. Butter both sides of each bread slice.
3. Spread the cream cheese mixture onto 4 slices of bread, then place a second slice of bread on top.
4. Heat a griddle or skillet over medium heat.
5. Dip each stuffed bread slice into the egg batter.
6. Place the battered bread slices onto the hot griddle and cook for about 4-5 minutes each side, until golden brown.
7. Serve with a dusting of powdered sugar and a drizzle of maple syrup. Enjoy!

Nutrition Information:

Serving Size 1 slice; Calories: 250; Total Fat: 11g; Saturated Fat: 5g; Cholesterol: 94mg; Sodium: 414mg; Total Carbohydrates: 30g; Dietary Fiber: 1g; Protein: 7g.

65. Apple Crumble

Apple Crumble – a delicious fruit-filled dessert, perfect for any occasion! Rich, buttery crumble is layered on top of a layer of baked apples for an irresistible sweet treat.
Serves: 8. Prep Time: 15 mins. | Ready Time: 45 mins.

Ingredients:
- 4 medium-sized apples of choice, peeled and sliced
- 3/4 cup light brown sugar
- 1/2 teaspoon ground cinnamon
- 2 teaspoons cornstarch
- 2/3 cup all-purpose flour
- 1/4 teaspoon salt
- 1/3 cup unsalted butter, cold and cubed

Instructions:
1. Preheat oven to 350F.
2. Grease an 8-inch square baking pan.
3. In a large bowl, toss together the sliced apples, 1/4 cup of the brown sugar, cinnamon and cornstarch.
4. Place apples in the greased baking pan and spread into an even layer.
5. In a separate bowl, combine the flour, remaining 1/2 cup of brown sugar, salt and cubed butter.
6. Use a fork or your fingers to work the butter into the flour mixture until it resembles course crumbs.
7. Sprinkle the crumble topping over the apples in the baking dish.
8. Bake for 35-40 minutes or until the topping is golden brown and the apples are tender.
9. Let cool before serving.

Nutrition Information:
Per Serving - Calories: 229, Fat: 9g, Carbohydrates: 36g, Protein: 2g, Sodium: 143mg, Sugar: 24g.

66. Chocolate Cake

This decadent and moist chocolate cake is perfect to satisfy your sweet tooth! It's the perfect dessert to bring to a gathering or to give as a special treat any day of the week.

Serving: 8
| Preparation Time: 30 minutes
| Ready Time: 1.5 hours

Ingredients:
- 2 cups all-purpose flour
- 2/3 cup cocoa powder
- 1 teaspoon baking soda
- 1/2 teaspoon salt
- 2/3 cup almond milk
- 1 teaspoon vanilla extract
- 1/2 cup vegetable oil or melted butter
- 1/2 cup boiling water
- 1.5 cups granulated sugar

Instructions:
1. Preheat the oven to 350F (175°C). Grease and flour one 9-inch round cake pan and set aside.
2. In a medium bowl, combine the flour, cocoa powder, baking soda and salt. In a separate bowl, whisk together the almond milk, oil/butter, vanilla extract and boiling water.
3. Pour the wet ingredients into the dry ingredients and mix until just combined.
4. Add the sugar and mix until just combined.
5. Pour the batter into the prepared cake pan and bake for 30-35 minutes or until a toothpick inserted into the center comes out clean.
6. Cool the cake in the pan for 10 minutes before turning out onto a cooling rack to cool completely.

Nutrition Information:

Calories: 284 kcal, Carbohydrates: 43 g, Protein: 3 g, Fat: 12 g, Saturated Fat: 5 g, Sodium: 206 mg, Potassium: 89 mg, Fiber: 2 g, Sugar: 28 g, Calcium: 33 mg, Iron: 1.2 mg.

67. Carrot Cake

Carrot cake is a classic dessert that's popular year-round. This moist, flavorful cake has a surprising blend of cinnamon, nutmeg and carrots, and a smooth cream cheese frosting that makes it impossible to resist.
Serving: 10
| Preparation Time: 30 minutes
| Ready Time: 1 hour 30 minutes

Ingredients:
- 2 cups all-purpose flour
- 2 teaspoons baking powder
- 1 teaspoon baking soda
- 1 teaspoon ground cinnamon
- 1/2 teaspoon freshly grated nutmeg
- 1/2 teaspoon kosher salt
- 1 1/2 cups granulated sugar
- 1 cup vegetable oil
- 3 large eggs
- 2 cups grated carrots
- 1/2 cup chopped walnuts (optional)
For the Cream Cheese Frosting:
- 4 ounces cream cheese, at room temperature
- 1/4 cup (1/2 stick) unsalted butter, at room temperature
- 2 cups powdered sugar
- 1 teaspoon freshly squeezed lemon juice

Instructions:
1. Preheat oven to 350F. Grease and flour two 9-inch round cake pans.
2. In a medium bowl, whisk together the flour, baking powder, baking soda, cinnamon, nutmeg, and salt.
3. In a large bowl, whisk together the sugar, oil, eggs and carrots. Add the dry ingredients to the wet ingredients and mix until combined. Fold in the walnuts, if using.

4. Divide the batter evenly between the prepared pans. Bake in preheated oven for 30 minutes, or until a toothpick inserted into the center of the cake comes out clean. Let cool in the pans for 10 minutes before removing to cooling racks to cool completely.

5. Make the cream cheese frosting by combining the cream cheese, butter, powdered sugar and lemon juice in a medium bowl and mixing until smooth.

6. Frost cooled cakes with the cream cheese frosting.

Nutrition Information: (per serving)
Calories: 372
Total Fat: 18 g
Saturated Fat: 7 g
Cholesterol: 51 mg
Sodium: 228 mg
Carbohydrates: 49 g
Fiber: 1 g
Sugar: 33 g
Protein: 4 g

68. Fruit Pizza

Fruit Pizza is a delicious and easy pizza recipe that can be enjoyed with the whole family. It is packed with fresh fruits, a tasty cream cheese topping, and a crispy sugar cookie crust. This pizza is ideal for an afternoon treat or dessert.

Serving: 8
| Preparation Time: 15 minutes
| Ready Time: 30 minutes

Ingredients:
• 1 package (1 lb) sugar cookies
• 1 package (8 oz) cream cheese, softened
• 1/3 cup sugar
• 1 teaspoon vanilla extract
• 2 cups assorted fresh fruit, such as kiwi, strawberries, and blueberries

Instructions:

1. Preheat oven to 350° F.
2. Place sugar cookies on an ungreased large round or rectangular pizza pan or baking sheet and bake for 8-10 minutes or until set.
3. Meanwhile, beat cream cheese with sugar and vanilla extract until light and fluffy.
4. Spread cream cheese mixture over cooled cookie.
5. Arrange fruit on top of the cream cheese.
6. Refrigerate for at least 30 minutes.

Nutrition Information:
Serving size: 1 slice | Calories: 270 | Fat: 10g | Saturated fat: 6g | Cholesterol: 25mg | Sodium: 180mg | Carbohydrates: 38g | Sugar: 26g | Protein: 4g

69. Monkey Bread

Monkey Bread is a classic pull apart sweet bread that is packed with brown sugar, cinnamon, and butter. Perfect for brunch or a cozy evening snack, this monkey bread recipe makes a delicious sticky treat!
Serving: 10
| Preparation Time: 20 minutes
| Ready Time: 45 minutes

Ingredients:
- 2 cans (16.3oz each) refrigerated biscuits
- 1/2 cup (1 stick) butter, melted
- 3/4 cup brown sugar
- 2 teaspoon ground cinnamon
- 1/2 cup pecans, chopped (optional)

Instructions:
1. Preheat oven to 350F. Grease a 9-inch round cake pan or Bundt pan.
2. Separate the biscuit dough into individual biscuits. Cut each biscuit into 4 smaller pieces.
3. In a medium bowl, mix together the melted butter, brown sugar, and cinnamon.

4. Place 1/3 of the biscuit pieces in the bottom of the cake pan. Top with 1/2 of the butter mixture. Sprinkle with 1/3 of the pecans, if desired.

5. Continue layering the remaining biscuit pieces, butter mixture and pecans.

6. Bake for 30-35 minutes, or until the monkey bread is golden brown and bubbly.

7. Allow to cool in the pan for 5-10 minutes. Invert onto a serving plate.

Nutrition Information:
Serving size: 1/10 of recipe
Calories: 299
Total Fat: 15g
Saturated Fat: 6g
Cholesterol: 17mg
Sodium: 590mg
Carbohydrates: 36g
Fiber: 1g
Sugar: 19g
Protein: 4g

70. Cheese Soufale

Cheese Soufflé is a classic French dish made with cheese, eggs, and seasonings that comes together to create a light and fluffy entrée. It's perfect for an indulgent brunch or dinner.
Serving: 4-6
| Preparation Time: 15 minutes
| Ready Time: 40 minutes

Ingredients:
• 4 tablespoons butter
• 8 ounces Gruyère cheese, grated
• 4 eggs, separated
• 1/4 teaspoon nutmeg
• 1/4 teaspoon cayenne pepper
• 3/4 cup heavy cream
• Salt and pepper to taste

Instructions:
1. Preheat oven to 375F. Grease four 4-ounce soufflé dishes with 1 tablespoon of butter each and place plates on baking sheets.
2. Melt remaining butter in a medium saucepan over medium heat. Add cheese and stir to combine until melted.
3. In a separate bowl, beat egg whites until stiff peaks form. In a medium bowl, beat egg yolks and slowly add melted cheese mixture.
4. Fold in egg whites, nutmeg and cayenne pepper.
5. Add cream and mix until everything is fully combined.
6. Pour mixture into the prepared soufflé dishes and bake for 35-40 minutes, until golden brown.
7. Serve immediately.

Nutrition Information (per serving):
Calories: 472
Fat: 35 g
Carbohydrates: 8.5 g
Protein: 30.3 g

71. Chocolate Chip Cookies

Who doesn't love a perfectly soft and gooey Chocolate Chip Cookie? This classic comfort food recipe is known by all and loved by many!
Serving: Makes 24 cookie
| Preparation Time: 15 minutes
| Ready Time: 30 minutes

Ingredients:
1. 2 1/8 cups all-purpose flour
2. 1 teaspoon baking soda
3. 1 teaspoon salt
4. 1 cup butter, softened
5. 3/4 cup granulated sugar
6. 3/4 cup packed light brown sugar
7. 2 teaspoons vanilla extract
8. 2 large eggs
9. 2 cups semisweet chocolate chips

Instructions:

1. Preheat oven to 375F.
2. In a medium bowl, stir together the flour, baking soda, and salt.
3. In a large bowl, beat the butter and sugars on medium-high speed until light and fluffy. Add the vanilla and eggs and beat until combined.
4. Gradually beat in the flour mixture until combined. Stir in the chocolate chips.
5. Spoon the cookie dough onto ungreased baking sheets, 2 inches apart. Bake for 8 to 10 minutes, until golden brown. Allow to cool on the baking sheets for a few minutes before transferring to a wire rack.

Nutrition Information:
Calories: 158 | Fat: 8.3g | Sodium: 148mg | Carbs: 21.1g | Fiber: 0.8g | Protein: 1.6g

72. Peanut Butter Cookies

Peanut Butter Cookies are a classic American favorite - the perfect balance of crunchy and chewy, and a great pairing for a cold glass of milk. These delicious treats are fast and easy to make, and can be ready in under 25 minutes!
Serving: Makes 24 small cookies
| Preparation Time: 10 minutes
| Ready Time: 15 minutes

Ingredients:
• 1 cup creamy peanut butter
• 3/4 cup sugar
• 1/4 cup light brown sugar
• 1 large egg
• 1 teaspoon baking soda
• 1 teaspoon vanilla extract

Instructions:
1. Preheat your oven to 350° F.

2. In a bowl, combine the peanut butter, sugars, egg, baking soda, and vanilla extract. Whisk together until the mixture is creamy.

3. Take a spoonful of the mixture at a time, and roll it into balls. Place the cookie balls onto a parchment-lined baking sheet.

4. Bake for 10-12 minutes, or until the cookies are golden-brown. Allow to cool for a few minutes before serving.

Nutrition Information (per serving):
Calories: 124.2, Fat: 6.3g, Carbohydrates: 14.3g, Protein: 3.3g

73. Brownies

Brownies are a classic rich and indulgent treat. They are perfect for treating a crowd, sharing at potlucks, or as an after dinner dessert. This recipe yields rich and fudge-like brownies.

Serving: 12
| Preparation Time: 10 minutes
| Ready Time: 25 minutes

Ingredients:
- 1/2 cup unsalted butter
- 1 cup granulated white sugar
- 2 large eggs
- 3/4 teaspoon pure vanilla extract
- 1/2 cup plus 1 tablespoon all-purpose flour
- 1/4 cup cocoa powder
- 1/2 teaspoon salt

Instructions:
1. Preheat oven to 350F (175°C). Grease an 8x8 inch baking pan.
2. In a large bowl, melt the butter in the microwave and stir in sugar until evenly mixed.
3. Beat in eggs, one at a time, then add the vanilla extract.
4. In a separate bowl, mix together the flour, cocoa powder, and salt.
5. Gradually add the dry ingredients to the wet ingredients and stir until completely combined.
6. Pour the batter into the prepared baking pan and bake for 25 minutes, until a toothpick inserted in the center comes out clean.

7. Let cool for 10 minutes before slicing and serving.

Nutrition Information (per serving):
231 Calories, 10 g Fat, 34 g Carbohydrates, 2 g Protein.

74. Key Lime Pie

Cool and creamy key lime pie is a classic Florida dessert featuring lime juice, cream cheese and condensed milk. It's a delightful summer treat that's perfect for entertaining.
Serving: 8-10
| Preparation Time: 20 minutes
| Ready Time: 5-6 hours

Ingredients:
- 25 regular-size graham cracker squares
- 2 tablespoons unsalted butter, melted
- 1 can (14 ounces) sweetened condensed milk
- 3 large limes (or 5-6 Key limes)
- 8 ounces full-fat cream cheese, at room temperature
- 1/2 cup granulated sugar

Instruction:
1. Preheat your oven to 350F. Place the graham crackers in a zip-top bag and use a rolling pin to crush them into crumbs until you have 2 cups. Add the melted butter and mix together until you have moist crumbs.
2. In a 9-inch pie dish, press the crumbs evenly into the bottom and up the sides of the dish. Bake for 10 minutes, until golden brown. Remove from the oven and cool completely.
3. In a medium bowl, add the condensed milk, the juice of the limes, the cream cheese, and the granulated sugar. Whisk together until very well blended.
4. Pour this mixture over the cooled graham cracker crust and spread it out evenly. Bake for 15 minutes, then cool for another 20 minutes. Chill in the refrigerator for at least 4 hours.

Nutrition Information:

Calories: 204, Protein: 4g, Carbs: 24g, Fat: 11g, Sugar: 21g, Sodium: 172mg, Fiber: 0g

75. Lemon Meringue Pie

Lemon Meringue Pie is an irresistible classic. It's smooth, tangy lemon filling offset by a fluffy and golden meringue topping creates a flavor combination that will make your mouth water. The perfect dessert for a special occasion or simply a treat!
Serving: 8-10
| Preparation Time: 25 minutes
| Ready Time: 2 hours

Ingredients:
- 1 pre-made 9-inch single pie crust
- 3/4 cup granulated sugar
- 2 tablespoons cornstarch
- 1/4 teaspoon salt
- 1 cup water
- 2 tablespoons butter
- 2 tablespoons freshly squeezed lemon juice
- 2 teaspoons grated lemon zest
- 2 egg yolks, beaten
- 4 egg whites
- 1/3 cup granulated sugar
- 1/4 teaspoon cream of tartar

Instructions:
1. Preheat the oven to 375F.
2. In a medium saucepan, add the sugar, cornstarch, salt, and water. Cook over medium heat until it comes to a boil. Then reduce the heat and simmer for a few minutes until it is thick and clear.
3. Remove from the heat and add the butter, lemon juice, and lemon zest. Stir until everything is well incorporated.
4. Place the saucepan back over low heat and add the egg yolks, stirring all the while. Continue cooking until it becomes thick and creamy.
5. Pour the filling into the pie crust, then set aside to cool while you make the meringue topping.

6. In a separate bowl, beat the egg whites until frothy, then add the sugar and cream of tartar. Continue to beat until it forms stiff peaks.
7. Place this meringue on the cooled pie, making sure to seal the edges. This will help to prevent the meringue from shrinking and leaking.
8. Bake for 15-20 minutes or until the top is golden.
9. When done, cool completely before serving.

Nutrition Information:
Each serving (1/8 of a 9-inch pie) contains 285 calories, 10.3 grams of fat, 46.2 grams of carbohydrates, and 5.3 grams of protein.

76. Tres Leches Cake

Tres Leches Cake is a traditional Mexican dessert of sponge cake soaked in three kinds of dairy, topped with whipped cream and fresh fruit. It is a frozen treat that pairs well with coffee and tea.
Serving: 8
| Preparation Time: 25 minutes
| Ready Time: 4-6 hours

Ingredients:
- 1 cup of all-purpose flour
- 2 teaspoons of baking powder
- 5 eggs
- 1 cup of sugar
- 1 teaspoon of vanilla extract
- a pinch of salt
- 12 ounces of evaporated milk
- 14 ounces of sweetened condensed milk
- 4 ounces of heavy cream
- 4 ounces of whipping cream
- 4 tablespoons of sugar
- Fresh fruit for topping (optional)

Instructions:
1. Preheat oven to 350F. Grease an 8x8 inch pan with butter.
2. In a medium bowl, whisk together flour and baking powder. Set aside.

3. In a separate bowl, beat together 5 eggs and 1 cup of sugar until light and fluffy. Slowly mix in the flour mixture, stirring until just combined. Stir in the vanilla extract and salt.

4. Pour batter into greased pan and bake in preheated oven for 25 minutes or until a toothpick inserted comes out clean.

5. In a medium bowl, whisk together evaporated milk, sweetened condensed milk, and heavy cream.

6. When the cake is done, poke several holes into the cake with a fork. Gradually pour the milk and cream mixture over the top of the cake, occasionally using a spoon to help spread the mixture evenly over the cake.

7. Refrigerate the cake for 4-6 hours until the cake has fully absorbed the liquid.

8. In a small bowl, whip the cream and 4 tablespoons of sugar together until thick and fluffy.

9. Spread the whipped cream over the top of the cake. Decorate the top with fresh fruits (optional).

Nutrition Information:
Serving Size: 1 slice (1/8th of the cake)
Calories: 300
Total Fat: 12g
Cholesterol: 98 mg
Sodium: 47mg
Total Carbohydrates: 37g
Protein: 8g

77. Almond Cake

Almond Cake is a classic dessert recipe made with almond flour, butter, eggs and sugar. It is wonderfully moist and fluffy and perfect for any occasion!
Serving: 8
| Preparation Time: 20 minutes
| Ready Time: 1 hour

Ingredients:
1.   11/2 cups (150g) almond flour

2. 1/2 teaspoon baking powder
3. Pinch of salt
4. 1/2 cup (115g) butter, at room temperature
5. 1 cup (200g) caster sugar
6. 2 large eggs
7. 2 tablespoons milk
8. 1 teaspoon almond extract

Instructions:
1. Preheat oven to 350F/175C. Grease a 9-inch round cake tin and line the base with parchment paper.
2. In a medium bowl, whisk together the almond flour, baking powder, and salt.
3. In a large bowl, use an electric mixer to beat the butter and sugar until light and creamy.
4. Beat in the eggs one at a time, then add the milk and almond extract.
5. Add the almond flour mixture and mix until combined.
6 Pour the batter into the prepared cake tin and bake for 35 minutes, or until a skewer inserted into the centre comes out clean.
7. Allow to cool in the tin before turning out onto a wire rack to cool completely.

Nutrition Information:
Serving Size: 1 Slice
Calories: 345 kcal
Total Fat: 17.9 g
Saturated Fat: 8.2 g
Cholesterol: 67.2 mg
Sodium: 107.7 mg
Total Carbohydrates: 40.7 g
Fiber: 1.7 g
Sugar: 24.7 g
Protein: 6.7 g

78. Zucchini Bread

Nothing refreshes the soul quite like the smell of warm, moist zucchini bread. Combining freshly grated zucchini and spices with buttermilk, and a touch of sweetness in the form of maple syrup, this zucchini bread is sure to be a hit with everyone.

Serving: Makes two 9x5-inch loaves, approximately 16-18 slices
| Preparation Time: 20 minutes
| Ready Time: 55 minutes

Ingredients:
- 2 1/2 cups all-purpose flour
- 2 teaspoons baking soda
- 1 teaspoon baking powder
- 3/4 teaspoon salt
- 1 teaspoon ground cinnamon
- 2 cups grated zucchini
- 1/2 cup vegetable oil
- 2 eggs
- 1/2 cup pure maple syrup
- 1/2 cup buttermilk
- 1/2 cup chopped walnuts (optional)

Instructions:
1. Preheat oven to 350F. Grease and flour two 9x5-inch loaf pans.
2. In a medium bowl, whisk together flour, baking soda, baking powder, salt, and cinnamon.
3. In a large bowl, combine zucchini, oil, eggs, maple syrup, and buttermilk.
4. Slowly add dry ingredients to wet ingredients and mix until combined. Optional to stir in walnuts.
5. Divide batter between two prepared loaf pans and spread evenly.
6. Bake for 45-55 minutes until a toothpick inserted in the center comes out clean.
7. Cool for 10 minutes in pans before moving to cooling rack to cool completely.

Nutrition Information:
Per slice (2 loafs): 194 Calories, 9 g Fat, 25 g Carbohydrates, 2 g Protein

79. Red Velvet Cupcakes

Red Velvet Cupcakes are a classic Southern dessert beloved for their moist, fluffy texture and true red velvet flavor. Filled with a sweet vanilla cream cheese frosting, these cupcakes will be the star of your next party!
Serving: 12 cupcakes
| Preparation Time: 30 minutes
| Ready Time: 2 hours

Ingredients:
1. 2 1/4 cups all-purpose flour
2. 2 tablespoons cocoa powder
3. 1 teaspoon baking soda
4. 1 1/4 cups vegetable oil
5. 1 cup sugar
6. 2 eggs
7. 1 cup buttermilk
8. 1 teaspoon white vinegar
9. 1 teaspoon vanilla extract
10. 1 teaspoon red food coloring, plus more for decoration

Instructions:
1. Preheat oven to 350 degrees F (175 degrees C). Line cupcake tin with 12 paper liners.
2. In a large bowl, whisk together the flour, cocoa powder and baking soda. In a separate bowl, mix together the oil and sugar until combined. Add eggs and mix until blended. Slowly pour in the buttermilk, vinegar and vanilla. Add the red food coloring until desired color is achieved.
3. Fold wet ingredients into the dry ingredients, stirring gently until everything is just combined. Scoop batter into cupcake liners and bake for 18-22 minutes, or until a toothpick inserted comes out clean. Allow to cool in the tin for 10 minutes before transferring to a cooling rack to cool completely.
4. Fill a piping bag with your favorite cream cheese frosting and pipe onto cupcakes. Add additional red food coloring and decorate as desired.

Nutrition Information:
Each cupcake has approximately 339 calories, 18 grams of fat, 41 grams of carbohydrates, and 4 grams of protein.

80. Chocolate Chip Banana Bread

This decadent Chocolate Chip Banana Bread is sure to please. With its delicious combination of bananas and chocolate chips, it is a sure crowd pleaser. Made with simple, healthy ingredients, it is a great choice for breakfast, snack or dessert.
Serving: Makes 1 loaf (12 slices)
| Preparation Time: 15 minutes
| Ready Time: 55 minutes

Ingredients:
-3 ripe bananas
-2 cups all-purpose flour
-1 teaspoon baking soda
-1 teaspoon baking powder
-1/2 teaspoon salt
-1/4 cup melted butter (or coconut oil)
-3/4 cup brown sugar
-2 eggs (or 1 flax egg)
-2 teaspoons vanilla extract
-1 cup semi-sweet chocolate chips

Instructions:
1. Preheat oven to 350F. Grease a 9x5 inch loaf pan and set aside.
2. In a medium bowl, mash the bananas until smooth.
3. In a large bowl, whisk together the flour, baking soda, baking powder and salt.
4. In a separate medium bowl, mix together the melted butter, brown sugar, eggs and vanilla extract.
5. Add the banana mixture to the wet ingredients, stirring until combined.
6. Slowly add the dry ingredients to the wet ingredients, stirring constantly until all the ingredients are just combined.
7. Gently fold in the chocolate chips.
8. Pour the batter into the prepared pan.
9. Bake in preheated oven for 45-50 minutes, or until a toothpick inserted in the center comes out clean.

Nutrition Information (per serving):
Calories: 217; Total Fat: 7g; Cholesterol: 36mg; Sodium: 168mg; Total Carbs: 33g; Fiber: 1g; Sugars: 18g; Protein: 3g

81. Apple Pie

Apple Pie is a classic, comforting dessert that's perfect for any occasion. A combination of apples, butter, and cinnamon, all sandwiched between two layers of flaky pastry, this delicious, home-baked treat is sure to please.
Serving: 8
| Preparation Time: 10 minutes
| Ready Time: 50 minutes

Ingredients:
-3 lbs apples (such as Granny Smith, Golden Delicious), peeled, cored, and thinly sliced
-1/2 cup sugar
-2 tablespoons all-purpose flour
-1 teaspoon ground cinnamon
-6 tablespoons butter, cold, cut into small pieces
-1/2 teaspoon freshly squeezed lemon juice
-Pastry for a double crust 9-inch pie
-1 tablespoon sugar
-1 tablespoon ground cinnamon

Instructions:
1. Preheat oven to 375 F.
2. In a medium bowl, toss together apples, sugar, flour, and cinnamon.
3. Place apple mixture in the bottom of the pie dish and dot with butter. Sprinkle lemon juice over the top.
4. Roll out the first crust and place over the apple mixture.
5. Cut off excess overhang. Crimp the edges together.
6. Roll out the second crust and place atop the pie. Cut off the excess overhang. Crimp the edges together or flute the edges. Cut several slits in the top crust for ventilation.
7. Sprinkle with the combined 1 tablespoon of sugar and 1 tablespoon of cinnamon.

8. Bake for 40-50 minutes, or until crust is golden brown and filling is bubbling.
9. Cool at least 1 hour before serving.

Nutrition Information:
Per Serving (1/8 of pie): 258 calories, 11.9g fat, 379.7mg sodium, 39.3g carbohydrate, 0.5g dietary fiber, 4.2g protein.

82. Pumpkin Spice Cake

This pumpkin spice cake is perfectly moist and flavorful. It has a great balance of pumpkin spices and sweetness, making it a wonderful dessert for the cooler seasons!
Serving: Makes 8 slices
| Preparation Time: 20 minutes
| Ready Time: 1 hour

Ingredients:
- 2 cups all-purpose flour
- 2 teaspoons baking powder
- 1 teaspoon cardamom
- 1/2 teaspoon pumpkin pie spice
- 1/4 teaspoon salt
- 1/4 cup butter, softened
- 3/4 cup white sugar
- 2 eggs
- 1 teaspoon vanilla extract
- 3/4 cup canned pumpkin puree
- 1/4 cup evaporated milk

Instructions:
1. Preheat oven to 350 degrees F (175 degrees C). Grease an 8-inch round baking dish.
2. In a medium bowl, sift together the flour, baking powder, cardamom, pumpkin pie spice and salt.
3. In a large bowl, cream together the butter and sugar until light and fluffy. Beat in the eggs one at a time, then mix in the vanilla. Mix in the pumpkin puree.

4. Add the flour mixture alternately with the evaporated milk to the pumpkin mixture, beating well after each addition.
5. Pour the batter into the prepared baking dish.
6. Bake for 30 minutes in the preheated oven, or until a knife inserted in the center comes out clean.

Nutrition Information:
Serving Size: 1 Slice
Calories: 180
Fat: 6 g
Cholesterol: 33 mg
Sodium: 122 mg
Potassium: 70 mg
Carbohydrates: 28 g
Fiber: 1 g
Sugar: 14 g
Protein: 4 g

83. Baked Apples

This delicious recipe for Baked Apples is a simple yet flavorful baked dessert that will tantalize the taste buds of any apple-lover. With only a few ingredients, this dish is perfect for a cozy evening indoors.
Serving: 4
| Preparation Time: 10 minutes
| Ready Time: 40 minutes

Ingredients:
- 4 apples, cored
- 1 tablespoon melted butter
- 2 tablespoons packed light brown sugar
- 1/4 teaspoon cinnamon
- 1/4 cup chopped walnuts

Instructions:
1. Preheat oven to 350F.
2. Core apples and place them in a baking dish.
3. Mix together melted butter, brown sugar, cinnamon and walnuts.

4. Fill the center of each apple with the butter-sugar mixture.
5. Bake in the preheated oven for 35-40 minutes, until apples are tender.

Nutrition Information (per serving):
Calories: 121 kcal
Fat: 6 g
Carbohydrates: 18 g
Protein: 1 g
Sodium: 1 mg

84. Chocolate Peppermint Bark

Chocolate Peppermint Bark is a decadent holiday treat that can be enjoyed by kids and adults alike. This melt-in-your mouth snack is made of semi-sweet chocolate, white chocolate and peppermint candy pieces – sure to get you in the holiday spirit!
Serving: 15
| Preparation Time: 5 minutes
| Ready Time: 30 minutes

Ingredients:
- 10 ounces semi-sweet chocolate chips
- 10 ounces white chocolate chips
- 4-5 candy canes, crush into small pieces

Instructions:
1. Line a baking sheet with parchment paper.
2. In a microwave-safe bowl, add semi-sweet chocolate chips and microwave for 1 minute. Remove from the microwave, stir and then microwave for an additional 15 seconds if needed.
3. Pour the melted chocolate onto the lined baking sheet, spreading it out in an even layer. Repeat the process with the white chocolate chips.
4. Sprinkle the crushed candy canes onto the chocolate layers.
5. Place the baking sheet in the freezer for 20-30 minutes or until fully hardened.
6. Break the chocolate bark into large pieces.

Nutrition Information (per serving):

Calories: 154
Total Fat: 9.5g
Cholesterol: 4.2mg
Sodium: 4.6mg
Total Carbohydrate: 18.2g
Dietary Fiber: 0.7g
Protein: 1.9g

85. Orange Creamsicle Cupcakes

Enjoy the classic flavors of a Creamsicle with these delicious Orange Creamsicle Cupcakes! Perfectly moist orange cake is paired with a creamy orange frosting to create a dessert that the whole family can enjoy.
Serving: 12 cupcakes
| Preparation Time: 20 minutes
| Ready Time: 1 hour

Ingredients:
- 1 cup all-purpose flour
- 1 1/2 teaspoons baking powder
- 1/2 teaspoon baking soda
- 1/4 teaspoon salt
- 1/4 cup butter, softened
- 1 cup sugar
- 2 eggs
- 1 tablespoon freshly grated orange zest
- 1 teaspoon vanilla extract
- 3/4 cup freshly squeezed orange juice
For the Frosting:
- 2 cups powdered sugar
- 4 tablespoons butter, softened
- 1 teaspoon orange zest
- 2 tablespoons freshly squeezed orange juice

Instructions:
1. Preheat oven to 350F and line cupcake pans with 12 cupcake liners.
2. In a medium bowl, whisk together flour, baking powder, baking soda, and salt.

3. In a large bowl, cream together butter and sugar until light and fluffy. Beat in the eggs, one at a time, followed by the orange zest and vanilla extract.
4. Add the dry ingredients in two batches, alternating with the orange juice.
5. Fill the cupcake liners halfway with the batter and bake for 18-20 minutes.
6. Allow cupcakes to cool completely before frosting.
7. For the frosting, beat the powdered sugar, butter, and orange zest together until combined. Slowly beat in the orange juice until smooth.
8. Pipe the frosting onto cooled cupcakes and garnish with freshly grated orange zest.

Nutrition Information:
Calories: 270; Fat: 8.3g; Carbs: 46.3g; Protein: 2.8g; Sodium: 237mg.

86. Strawberry Tiramisu

This Strawberry Tiramisu is a delicious, light and fluffy Italian dessert with layers of ladyfingers, creamy mascarpone filling and fresh strawberries! It is perfect for any occasion, from a fancy dinner party to a casual get-together with friends.
Serving: Serves 4-6
| Preparation Time: 20 minutes
| Ready Time: 2 hours

Ingredients:
- 16 ounces mascarpone
- 2 1/2 cups heavy cream
- 1/4 cup sifted powder sugar
- 2 tablespoons pure vanilla extract
- 2 tablespoons organic cornstarch
- 12 ounces ladyfingers
- 2 cups unsweetened fresh strawberries, diced
- 1/4 cup strawberry jam
- Powdered sugar

Instructions:

1. In a large bowl, cream together mascarpone and heavy cream using a stand mixer or a whisk.
2. Add in powdered sugar, vanilla extract, and cornstarch and mix until combined.
3. In the bottom of a springform pan, layer half of the ladyfingers.
4. Spread half of the strawberry jam over the ladyfingers.
5. Top with half of the mascarpone mixture and spread gently.
6. Add a layer of fresh diced strawberries.
7. Layer the remaining ladyfingers, jam and mascarpone mixture.
8. Refrigerate for two hours to set.
9. Dust with powdered sugar before serving.

Nutrition Information:
Per serving (1/6 of the recipe): 420 calories, 31g fat, 21g carbohydrates, 6g protein.

87. Caramel Brownies

These fudgy and gooey Caramel Brownies are guaranteed to become your new favorite dessert! With a layer of rich chocolatey brownie and a layer of sweet, creamy caramel, they are the perfect balance of flavors.
Serving: 16
| Preparation Time: 15 Minutes
| Ready Time: 1 hour

Ingredients:
- 3/4 cup unsalted butter
- 2 cups sugar
- 3 large eggs
- 1 teaspoon vanilla extract
- 2/3 cup all-purpose flour
- 1/4 teaspoon fine sea salt
- 1/2 cup cocoa powder
- 1/2 cup semi-sweet chocolate chips
- 1/2 cup caramel sauce

Instructions:
- Preheat oven to 350° F (177° C).

- Grease a 9x13 inch baking pan.
- In a medium bowl, combine the flour, salt, and cocoa powder, stir until combined.
- In a larger bowl, cream the butter and sugar until light and fluffy.
- Add the eggs one at a time, beating well after each addition.
- Add the vanilla extract and mix to combine.
- Gradually add the flour mixture, stirring until just combined.
- Pour the batter into the prepared baking dish.
- Sprinkle the chocolate chips evenly over the brownie batter.
- Pour the caramel sauce over the top.
- Bake for 35-40 minutes, until a toothpick inserted into the center comes out clean.
- Allow the brownies to cool in the pan before cutting into bars.

Nutrition Information:
Serving size: 1, Calories: 282, Total fat: 17g, Saturated fat: 10g, Cholesterol: 70mg, Sodium: 81mg, Carbohydrates: 32g, Fiber: 1g, Sugar: 24g, Protein: 2g

88. Coconut Pound Cake

This Coconut Pound Cake is a delicious and sweet dessert that is sure to please everyone. It is made with coconut flakes, sugar, butter, eggs and all-purpose flour, making it a quick and easy treat that can be enjoyed whenever.
Servings: 8
| Preparation Time: 10 minutes
| Ready Time: 1 hour

Ingredients:
- 1 cup unsalted butter, at room temperature
- 1 cup granulated sugar
- 3 large eggs
- 2 cups all-purpose flour
- 1 teaspoon baking powder
- 1/2 teaspoon salt
- 1/4 cup coconut flakes
- 1 teaspoon pure vanilla extract

Instructions:
1. Preheat the oven to 350F. Grease an 8" round pan and set aside.
2. In the bowl of a stand mixer, cream together the butter and sugar until light and fluffy.
3. Add eggs one at a time, mixing until each one is fully incorporated.
4. In a separate bowl, whisk together the flour, baking powder, and salt.
5. Add the dry ingredients to the wet ingredients, mixing until just combined.
6. Stir in the coconut flakes and vanilla extract.
7. Transfer the batter to the prepared pan. Bake for 45 minutes or until a skewer inserted into the center comes out clean.
8. Allow the cake to cool before serving.

Nutrition Information:
Per serving (1/8th of cake): Calories 440, Fat 18g, Carbohydrates 64g, Protein 5g, Sodium 200mg.

89. Chocolate Eclairs

Chocolate Eclairs are decadent, twice-baked French pastries filled with creamy custard and topped with a rich chocolate ganache. Serve these decadent desserts and they will be devoured in minutes!
Serving: 8
| Preparation Time: 45 minutes
| Ready Time: 3 hours

Ingredients:
-2 1/2 cups all-purpose flour
-1 teaspoon salt
-1 cup (2 sticks) butter
-1 cup water
-2 tablespoons sugar
-4 eggs
-1 (8-ounce) package cream cheese, at room temperature
-1 cup confectioners' sugar
-1 teaspoon pure vanilla extract
-1 cup heavy cream

-1 (4-ounce) package semisweet chocolate chips

Instructions:
1. Preheat oven to 400 degrees F.
2. In a bowl, sift together the flour and salt. Set aside.
3. In a medium saucepan, combine the butter, water, and sugar. Heat over medium heat, stirring occasionally, until the butter is melted and the sugar is dissolved.
4. Add the flour mixture to the pan and stir with a wooden spoon until the mixture forms a ball and pulls away from the sides of the pan. Remove from heat and allow to cool for 10 minutes.
5. Transfer the mixture to a large bowl. Using an electric mixer, beat in the eggs one at a time until the mixture is light and fluffy.
6. Line a baking sheet with parchment paper then drop 8 large spoonfuls of the batter onto the parchment paper and bake for 15 minutes.
7. Remove from the oven and allow to cool. Once cool, split the eclairs open and set aside.
8. To make the filling, beat together the cream cheese, confectioners' sugar and vanilla until light and fluffy.
9. In a medium bowl, whip the cream until stiff peaks form. Gently fold the whipped cream into the cream cheese mixture.
10. Spoon the filling into the eclairs and set aside.
11. In a microwave-safe bowl, heat the chocolate chips in 30 second intervals, stirring in between, until the chocolate is melted and smooth.
12. Drizzle the melted chocolate over the top of the eclairs and serve.

Nutrition Information:
Calories: 148, Total Fat: 8.9g, Saturated Fat: 5.4g, Cholesterol: 34mg, Sodium: 199mg, Potassium: 10mg, Total Carbohydrates: 16.1g, Dietary Fiber: 0.5g, Sugars: 3.2g, Protein: 2.2g.

90. Orange Upside Down Cake

This moist and delicious Orange Upside Down Cake is a stunning citrusy showstopper that's surprisingly easy to make and sure to be a tasty hit.
Serving: 8-10
| Preparation Time: 15 minutes
| Ready Time: 1 hour

Ingredients:
-1/2 cup butter, melted
-3/4 cup brown sugar
-1 orange, sliced into rounds
-1/2 cup all-purpose flour
-1 tsp baking powder
-1/4 tsp salt
-2 eggs
-1/2 cup white sugar
-1 tsp orange zest
-1/2 cup freshly squeezed orange juice

Instructions:
1. Preheat oven to 350 degrees F. Grease a 9-inch cake pan.
2. In a small bowl, mix together melted butter and brown sugar. Pour into cake pan and spread evenly over bottom. Place orange slices on top of sugar in a single layer.
3. In a medium bowl, combine flour, baking powder and salt. In a separate bowl, beat eggs with white sugar, orange zest and orange juice until smooth.
4. Slowly add flour mixture to egg mixture, beating until just combined. Spread batter over oranges in cake pan.
5. Bake for 40-45 minutes, until golden brown and a toothpick inserted in the center comes out clean.
6. Let cool in pan for 15 minutes, then invert onto serving plate. Enjoy!

Nutrition Information:
Calories: 204 (per slice); Fat: 8g; Cholesterol: 48mg; Sodium: 139mg; Carbohydrate: 30g; Fiber: 1g; Sugar: 23g; Protein: 2g

91. Raspberry Cheesecake Bars

These indulgent Raspberry Cheesecake Bars boast a sweet graham cracker crust with a creamy, tangy cheesecake layer, topped off with a fresh raspberry topping. This crowd-pleasing dessert is sure to have everyone clamouring for seconds!
Serving: 24 bars

| Preparation Time: 15 minutes
| Ready Time: 2 hours

Ingredients:
- 2 cups graham cracker crumbs
- 1/2 cup butter, melted
- 2 (8 oz) packages cream cheese, softened
- 1 cup granulated sugar
- 2 Large eggs
- 1 teaspoon vanilla extract
- 2 cups fresh raspberries

Instructions:
1. Preheat oven to 325F. Line a 9x13 inch baking dish with aluminum foil, leaving some foil overhanging on each side.
2. In a medium bowl, mix together graham cracker crumbs and melted butter until evenly combined. Press mixture into the bottom of the prepared baking dish.
3. In a separate bowl, using an electric mixer, beat together cream cheese and sugar until light and fluffy. Add in eggs, one at a time, beating until just combined. Add vanilla extract and beat until combined. Spread cream cheese mixture on top of graham cracker crust.
4. Place raspberries on top of cream cheese layer. Bake for 35-40 minutes until golden brown. Cool completely before slicing and serving.

Nutrition Information:
Per serving (1 bar): Calories 168, Fat 8 g, Saturated Fat 5 g, Cholesterol 37 mg, Sodium 156 mg, Total Carbohydrate 21 g, Dietary Fiber 1 g, Sugars 11 g, Protein 3 g.

92. Peach Cobbler

With a layer of spiced and buttery biscuit topping, this Peach Cobbler is a sweet and delicious dessert.
Serving: 8-10
| Preparation Time: 10 minutes
| Ready Time: 45 minutes

Ingredients:
-4 cups ripe peaches, sliced
-2 tablespoons fresh lemon juice
-1/2 cup unsalted butter
-1/4 cup granulated sugar
-1/4 cup light brown sugar
-1/4 teaspoon ground cinnamon
-1/4 teaspoon ground nutmeg
-2 tablespoons cornstarch
-1 cup all-purpose flour
-2 teaspoons baking powder
-1/2 teaspoon salt
-1/2 cup milk

Instructions:
1. Preheat the oven to 375 degrees F/190 degrees C.
2. In a large bowl, combine the peaches and lemon juice, stirring well to mix.
3. Spread the peach mixture evenly in an 8x10-inch baking dish.
4. In a small saucepan over low heat, melt the butter, then add both sugars, cinnamon, and nutmeg, stirring until the sugars are dissolved.
5. In a small bowl, combine the cornstarch and a few tablespoons of the butter mixture, stirring until smooth.
6. Pour the cornstarch mixture into the saucepan and simmer, stirring, until thickened (about 2 minutes).
7. Pour the butter mixture over the peaches in the baking dish.
8. In a medium bowl, combine the flour, baking powder, and salt.
9. Add the milk and mix until a dough forms.
10. Drop spoonfuls of the dough evenly over the top of the peach mixture.
11. Bake for 25 minutes, until the cobbler is golden brown.
12. Serve warm.

Nutrition Information:
Per Serving (8 oz/227 g): Calories 250, Total Fat 12g (Saturated 5g, Trans 0.5g), Cholesterol 20mg, Sodium 310mg, Total Carbohydrate 34g (Dietary Fiber 2g, Sugars 17g), Protein 3g.

93. Rice Pudding

Rice pudding is a comforting and delicious dessert that can be enjoyed by everyone. This classic recipe combines long-grain white rice with sweetened condensed milk, cinnamon, and raisins for an irresistible treat.
Serving: 4-6 people
| Preparation Time: 15 minutes
| Ready Time: 45 minutes

Ingredients:
1. 2 cups uncooked long-grain white rice
2. 1 (14-ounce) can sweetened condensed milk
3. 2 cups milk
4. 1 teaspoon ground cinnamon
5. 1/4 cup raisins

Instructions:
1. In a medium saucepan, bring 2 cups of water to a boil. Add the rice and stir until the water boils again. Reduce the heat and simmer, uncovered, for 12 minutes.
2. Remove the rice from the heat and add the sweetened condensed milk, milk, and cinnamon. Stir until completely combined.
3. Return the saucepan to medium heat and bring to a simmer. Simmer the mixture for 25 minutes, stirring occasionally.
4. Stir in the raisins and cook for an additional 5 minutes.
5. Remove from heat and let sit for 10 minutes. Serve warm and enjoy!

Nutrition Information (per serving):
Calories:261
Fat: 4 g
Carbohydrates:48 g
Protein:7 g

94. Cannoli

Cannoli is a decadent and delicious Italian pastry that consists of a fried pastry shell filled with a sweet and creamy ricotta cheese mixture.
Servings: 6 | Preparation Time: 1 hour | Ready Time: 1.5 hours.

Ingredients:
- 375g cannoli shells
- 225g ricotta cheese
- 70g caster sugar
- 50g mini chocolate chips
- 2 tsp vanilla extract
- Optional garnish - icing sugar and chopped pistachios

Instructions:
1. Preheat oven to 180°C/350°F and place cannoli shells on a prepared baking sheet in an even layer and bake for 10 minutes, until lightly golden brown.
2. Meanwhile, in a large mixing bowl, use an electric mixer to mix together the ricotta cheese, sugar, chocolate chips, and vanilla extract until light and creamy.
3. When the cannoli shells have finished baking, remove from the oven and let cool completely.
4. Once the cannoli shells are cool, carefully spoon the ricotta mixture into them until filled, and garnish as desired.

Nutrition Information:
Total Calories: 280, Total Fat: 5.6g, Saturated Fat: 1.2g, Trans Fat 0g, Cholesterol: 9.5mg, Sodium: 175mg, Total Carbohydrates: 49g, Dietary Fiber: 1.4g, Total Sugars: 28g, Protein: 7.4g.

95. Apple Dumplings

Introducing Apple Dumplings - an easy-to-make dessert that everyone will love. This recipe uses cinnamon, butter, and apples to create a comforting and delicious treat.
Serving: 6-8
| Preparation Time: 15 minutes
| Ready Time: 45 minutes

Ingredients:
- 2 Granny Smith apples
- 2 tablespoons of butter

- 1/4 cup of dark brown sugar
- 2 teaspoons of cinnamon
- 2 cups of all-purpose flour
- 6 tablespoons of cold butter
- 2 tablespoons of granulated sugar
- 2 tablespoons of baking powder
- 1 teaspoon of salt
- 1/2 teaspoon of vanilla extract
- 1/2 cup of milk
- 2 tablespoons of melted butter

Instructions:
1. Preheat oven to 375F.
2. Peel apples and cut into 1/2-inch cubes.
3. In a large bowl, add butter, dark brown sugar, and cinnamon. Mix until fully combined.
4. Add apples and toss until the apples are fully coated.
5. In a separate bowl, whisk together flour, 2 tablespoons of granulated sugar, baking powder, and salt. Cut in 6 tablespoons of butter until the mixture resembles coarse crumbs.
6. Stir in milk and vanilla extract until the dough comes together.
7. On a lightly floured surface, roll out the dough into a 10-inch square.
8. Transfer the apple mixture onto the dough, leaving a 1-inch border.
9. Fold the dough to cover the apples. Brush the dough with melted butter.
10. Top with remaining granulated sugar and cinnamon. Cut into 8 pieces.
11. Place onto baking sheet. Bake for 35-40 minutes.

Nutrition Information (per serving):
230 Calories, 10g Fat, 29g Carbohydrates, 2g Protein

96. Blueberry Cobbler

This delicious blueberry cobbler is simple to make and incredibly delicious! This cobbler is best served warm with a scoop of ice cream or a dollop of whipped cream.
Serving: Serves 8

Ingredients:
• 2 sticks (1 cup) butter, melted and cooled
-4 cups fresh blueberries
-2 cups sugar, divided
-2 cups all-purpose flour
-1 teaspoon baking powder
-1 teaspoon baking soda
-1 teaspoon salt
-1 cup milk

Instructions:
1. Preheat oven to 375F.
2. Grease a 9x13 inch baking dish.
3. In a medium bowl, combine the melted butter, 1 cup of sugar, flour, baking powder, baking soda, and salt.
4. Place the blueberries in the greased baking dish.
5. Sprinkle the remaining 1 cup of sugar over the blueberries.
6. Pour the milk over the blueberries.
7. Top the blueberries with the dry ingredient mixture.
8. Bake in preheated oven for 40-45 minutes, or until the top is golden brown.

Nutrition Information (per serving):
Calories: 351, Total Fat: 14g, Saturated Fat: 9g, Cholesterol: 44mg, Sodium: 277mg, Total Carbohydrates: 55g, Dietary Fiber: 2g, Sugars: 36g, Protein: 4g.

97. Bananas Foster

Bananas Foster is a classic dessert consisting of caramelized bananas served atop a creamy, custard sauce. It is a sweet, delicious and unique way to enjoy fresh bananas.
Serving: 4-6
| Preparation Time: 5 minutes
| Ready Time: 10 minutes

Ingredients:
- 4 to 6 bananas
- 2 tablespoons butter
- 1/2 cup dark brown sugar
- 1/4 teaspoon ground cinnamon
- 1/4 cup dark rum
- Vanilla ice cream

Instructions:
1. Peel and slice the bananas into 1/2 inch rounds.
2. Heat the butter on medium heat in a large skillet. Add the bananas and cook for 1 minute.
3. Add in the dark brown sugar and cinnamon and cook until the sugar is dissolved.
4. Pour in the rum and bring to a boil. Boil for 1 minute, stirring constantly.
5. Remove the pan from the heat and serve over vanilla ice cream.

Nutrition Information:
Per Serving:
Calories: 239 kcal | Carbohydrates: 47.2g | Protein: 0.9g | Fat: 4.3g | Sodium: 71mg | Sugar: 35.2g

98. Pineapple Upside Down Cake

This decadent Pineapple Upside Down Cake is a classic Southern recipe, with caramelized pineapple nestled in a traditional rum cake, and topped with a delicious cream cheese glaze.
Serving
This cake will serve 8.
| Preparation Time
30 minutes.
Ready Time
1 hour.

Ingredients
1. 2 tablespoons butter, softened
2. 1/2 cup packed dark brown sugar

3. 1 pineapple, sliced
4. 1 cup granulated sugar
5. 2 eggs
6. 1 teaspoon baking powder
7. 1/2 teaspoon baking soda
8. 1/4 teaspoon salt
9. 1 teaspoon ground cinnamon
10. 1/2 cup buttermilk
11. 1/2 cup vegetable oil
12. 1 teaspoon vanilla extract
13. 1-1/2 cups all-purpose flour

Instructions

1. Preheat oven to 350°. Grease a 9-inch round cake pan and place the butter in it; sprinkle with the brown sugar. Arrange the pineapple slices in a single layer over the butter and brown sugar.
2. In a large bowl, whisk together the granulated sugar, eggs, baking powder, baking soda, salt, and cinnamon until well combined. Pour in the buttermilk, oil, and vanilla; whisk until blended. Gradually add the flour, whisking until a smooth batter forms.
3. Pour the batter over the pineapple and bake until a toothpick inserted in the center comes out with moist crumbs, 40–45 minutes. Let the cake cool in the pan for 15 minutes before inverting onto a serving platter.

Nutrition Information

Per serving (1/8 of cake): Calories 370, Fat 19g, Cholesterol 47mg, Sodium 324mg, Carbohydrate 47g, Fiber 1g, Sugar 31g, Protein 4g.

CONCLUSION

The cookbook 98 Delicious Food Processor Recipes: Quick and Easy Meals for Every Occasion is an invaluable source of guidance and inspiration for anyone looking to save time, money and effort in the kitchen. With a broad range of recipes, it offers something for everyone, no matter their cooking level. The range of ingredients is also broad, making this cookbook the perfect choice for anyone on a budget.

The most appealing aspect is the emphasis on speed and ease. Every recipe is designed to be quick and convenient, but each of them also produces delicious results. Even the most inexperienced cook will soon find their confidence in the kitchen growing. The book is also accompanied by easy-to-follow photographs and illustrations, which make the tasks much easier to complete.

This cookbook is a great buy for those who want to make delicious and nutritious meals without spending hours in the kitchen. The recipes are varied and include something for every occasion, making this book the ideal choice for busy households. Furthermore, the nutritional value of each meal has been included, meaning no dish could ever be considered unhealthy.

In short, this cookbook is an ideal addition to any kitchen. Whether a beginner or a seasoned cook, 98 Delicious Food Processor Recipes: Quick and Easy Meals for Every Occasion is a fantastic companion for anyone seeking tasty and nutritious fare. For anyone looking to save time, effort and money while achieving delicious results, this cookbook is an excellent choice.

Printed in Great Britain
by Amazon

42548180R00066